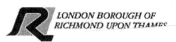

THE LITTLE GIRL
ON THE ICE FLOE

Adélaïde Bon

THE LITTLE GIRL
ON THE ICE FLOE

Translated from the French by
Ruth Diver

MACLEHOSE PRESS
QUERCUS · LONDON

First published in the French language as
La petite fille sur la banquise by Editions Grasset & Fasquelle, Paris, in 2018

First published in Great Britain in 2019 by MacLehose Press

MacLehose Press
An imprint of Quercus Publishing Ltd
Carmelite House
50 Victoria Embankment
London EC4Y ODZ

An Hachette UK company

This book is supported by the Institut français (Royaume-Uni)
as part of the Burgess programme

INSTITUT
FRANÇAIS
ROYAUME-UNI

Excerpt from "When evil-doing comes like falling rain", *Bertolt Brecht:
Poems 1913–1956*, ed. John Willett and Ralph Manheim, translated by John
Willett, Routledge 2007

A CIP catalogue record for this book is available from the British Library.

ISBN (HB) 978 0 85705 955 0
ISBN (TPB) 978 0 85705 954 3
ISBN (Ebook) 978 0 85705 957 4

1 3 5 7 9 10 8 6 4 2

Designed and typeset in Cycles by Libanus Press, Marlborough
Printed and bound in Great Britain by Clays Ltd, Elcograf S.p.A.

For Doctor Muriel Salmona,

for the long-haul investigator,

for all victims of violence,

my heroines.

When crimes begin to pile up they become invisible. When sufferings become unendurable the cries are no longer heard. The cries, too, fall like rain in summer.

BERTOLT BRECHT

DID SHE WIPE HER MOUTH with the back of her hand, run her tongue over her teeth, tidy her hair a bit? Was it her or him who pulled up her knickers, straightened her red pinafore dress, tucked in her white blouse? She looks at him, nodding like one of those little dogs on the back ledges of cars. "I'm a good girl, I'm pretty, I like it, you're my friend, you like my big bottom, you're nice to me, I'm greedy, I won't tell anyone, it's our secret, I promise you, I won't tell." Words he said to her and which she doesn't remember, just as she doesn't remember what he did to her.

She picks up the white paper bag of Carambar toffees and the container of goldfish flakes she had put down on the naked corner of a step.

Something has toppled over, she can't work out whether it's the floor or her, she needs to concentrate to climb the stairs.

She turns round on the landing when he calls her, promises again by nodding her head.

*

She is lying on her bed, she tries to catch a tear with the tip of her tongue. The floorboards in the hallway creak, she grabs her book. *Nobody's Child*, by Hector Malot.

"Is the book making you cry?" her father asks, no doubt alarmed that she slipped from the front door to her bedroom like a shadow, without the ritual booming "Hello my dear family I love and cherish", without slamming the door to the apartment, without coming to tell them anything.

Her head moves. Left. Right. Right. Left.

"Has something happened?"

Her head moves. Up. Down. Down. Up.

She is sitting between her parents on the maroon sofa in the living room, her brother and sisters have disappeared. She looks at the walls covered in fabric, she doesn't recognise them, just as she doesn't recognise her own parents. Everything has changed suddenly, but she can't understand what. They talk to her, she struggles to hear them, to understand them. She's floating.

She is sitting in the back of the police car, next to her father. The policemen put on the flashing lights to make her smile. She smiles. She is a good girl. She is no longer there. She is dead. No-one seems to realise.

At the police station, a policewoman asks her questions, she must answer yes or no, she nods or shakes her head accordingly. She feels nothing. The policewoman notes, "He touched my bottom: front and back. He took my left hand and put it on his willy."

They tell her she is "reporting unwanted sexual contact" and that the man in the stairwell is a "paedophile". She nods.

She does not feel the jellyfish slither into her that day, doesn't feel their long transparent tentacles penetrate her, doesn't know that their venomous filaments will gradually drag her into a story that is not her own, that is not about her. She doesn't know that they will cast her off her path, draw her down into deserted and inhospitable depths, obstruct her every step, make her doubt her strength, shrink the world around her, year after year, to a little air pocket with no way out. She doesn't know that she is at war now, and the enemy army is living inside her.

Nobody warns her, nobody explains this to her, the world has gone quiet.

The years will pass. They will forget that sunny Sunday in May, or rather, they will never speak of it again. And she will never think about it either.

OF COURSE, BEFORE THAT, you'd had your share of fights, sadness, anger, defeats and funerals. You had already learned that loving someone with all your might doesn't stop them from dying, but you can continue to talk to them afterwards, just like you used to talk to Grand-Père, under the plum tree. You knew there were illnesses that no-one recovers from and questions to which there are no answers. But answers were there in the spiderwebs sparkling with dew that no words could contain. God lived in the depths of your heart and in the buzzing of insects in spring-time. You climbed up to the tops of trees to feel yourself sway with them in the breeze. You had a boyfriend who was a fencer and you drew him a picture of the twelve children you would have together one day. You would throw earth-shattering tantrums and sit down on the pavement and flatly refuse to get up. You used to collect pretty words and crazy words in your notebooks. You wanted to become a firefighter, to save the world, to be a great writer. You couldn't care less about mirrors and appearances. You were nine years old.

I

THE NEXT DAY, SHE TELLS her boyfriend about it. The bell rings at the end of playtime, they are standing next to her desk – I can't quite remember what she said, what words she used – she sensed that nothing would ever feel the same again, and she ought to tell him. She doesn't wait for his answer, she goes and sits down, nice and straight.

She starts eating more, she was greedy before – I don't know whether she realises it, but from now on she will no longer eat for sustenance, but to calm herself down.

She has everything she needs to be happy. She has a very privileged, sheltered childhood. She is in good health, she is pretty, she is intelligent. She lives in Paris. She skis in the winters, swims in the summers, and visits museums abroad. She is from a good family living in a fine neighbourhood, she is well brought up, she knows how to behave in company. She is white, French since the time of Morvan I, King of the Bretons, and Charlemagne, raised in the Catholic faith and to have concern for others. One of her grandfathers was a decorated war hero, fallen for France. Her father has made a success of his life, her mother too. Parents with fascinating, responsible, high-profile professions, with a hectic and fulfilling social life. Parents who are busy, awkward, tender and profoundly loving.

When she is alone, she talks with an enormous white yeti, which only she can see, and with Pandi Panda, her old bear from China. They protect her, reassure her, and when she is with them, she can settle herself. She still sucks her thumb. Sometimes she grabs the yeti's hand, on the street, or when there are too many people around and she just can't keep track of them all by herself.

Some days, the objects around her hold conversations and she can spend a whole hour in the bathroom, immobile, listening to them talking inside her head.

Some nights, year after year, she is dreaming, then something interrupts the unfolding of her dream, something, a particular place she notices on her body that starts spinning, spinning faster and faster, the whirlwind grows bigger and sucks her in, the edges of her body crumble away, they disappear little by little, she cannot turn her eyes away, her body is a sandy desert that swirls and sinks, the sand is squishy, it fills her mouth, nothing to hold on to, she slips, she dissolves, and when the whirl-wind has taken over all the space in the dream, when she is about to disappear, she screams. She wakes up with a start. She listens. She is frightened that she might have actually screamed, might have woken her parents. There is something horribly dirty in this dream, something that she must not talk about.

IN THE SPRING OF THE following year, she is ten years old and has a white hooded T-shirt. She is happy to get away from round collars and smocked frocks for once. One of the show-off girls from the playground elite compliments her on her outfit, and her heart suddenly fills with delight, her heart overflows, she always feels so useless so ugly so fat, she doesn't even know how to look at herself anymore except through other people's eyes.

At a friend's birthday party, everyone is playing hide-and-seek. Her boyfriend pulls her behind one of the heavy curtains in the living room. They look at each other, she blushes, he moves his little lips closer, she's short of breath, she shuts her eyes and suddenly, she freezes. Something has slipped into her and grabbed her, a disgusting thing, a sensation throughout her whole body, a chill that is too terrifying to describe.

Disappointed, he goes to find another girl to kiss.

*

Her mother takes her to an aunt who is a nutritionist; she has gained a lot of weight. She must record everything she eats in a little notebook, but there are things she would rather not write down, quantities she doesn't mention. She's the one who finishes everybody's plates when nobody is looking, who gobbles up the leftovers instead of throwing them away, who is the first one up to clear the table, who is always smiling, always ready to lend a hand, always running to the kitchen to stuff herself until she goes numb.

As the days pass, the jellyfish multiply.

Her mother takes her to a large police station on the banks of the Seine. The police officers hand her a file crammed full of photographs of men, she has to look at them carefully, one by one. She would like to be able to say, "that's him", but none of these anonymous faces are familiar, none of them remind her of anything. She doesn't dare ask whether all these men, all these hundreds of paper men looking at her, are "paedophiles" too.

In *sixième*, the history teacher asks volunteers to give presentations about a period of their choice. She chooses the Holocaust. She spends hours in the local library, looking at kindly skeletons in striped pyjamas with lifeless eyes, offering their toothless smiles to the Red

Army photographers. She doesn't tell her parents she has borrowed "Night and Fog", she waits until she is alone one afternoon to watch it. Her presentation is so detailed that it stretches over four class periods and the history teacher is so worried she talks to her parents.

She is lively and cheerful when she's in company, and as soon as no-one is watching, she eats. She still laughs, maybe even more than before – her heart is just so heavy that when joy comes to find her, she dives deep into it.

She goes back with her mother to the large police station by the Seine. A policeman shows her into a dark room: on the other side of a partition that is partly glass, five men with closed faces are lined up in front of her, looking at her. She is very frightened. The policeman reassures her, "It's a two-way mirror, they can't see you."

She doesn't understand, "a 2A mirror", she forces herself to smile, to come closer to the glass, to stare at the men. She wishes she could be helpful, but she still doesn't recognise any of those faces.

That day, or maybe another time, she has to describe the face of the man in the stairwell. "What was the shape of his face? Oval, long? And his hairline?" On the screen of the big grey computer, they scroll through a strange catalogue of separate parts, chins, noses, eyes, foreheads, cheeks, mouths, ears, eyebrows, so that in the end, after a long joint effort, a face appears, a strange sort of face, a corpse's face, a nobody face, a nothing face. Another face she doesn't recognise.

She receives a Catholic education, from which she retains the Devil and his temptations, sin, the omniscient eye of God fixed upon her, Hell. She hears about the hatred of the body and the rejection of the senses in sermons about the primacy of the spirit. This reassures her. She despises her body and feels as though it is an imposed vessel, a cesspit. She hopes to have a pure and virginal soul, united with God, dismembered from this body where Satan dwells.

She often masturbates, in the Latin sense, *manus stupratio*, she soils herself with her hand. She doesn't remember when it started or where the movements came from, always the same ones. She doesn't know what to call them. All it takes is for her to be alone, then the Devil comes to her and goes down into her pants. So she hits her vulva, mechanically, compulsively, until it is inflamed and sore, until she falls into a numb, jelly-like stupor. She doesn't tell anyone about it, she knows it's bad, she just can't stop herself. She needs the floaty feeling that comes afterwards. In church, she avoids looking into the hollow eyes of the little devils sculpted on the column capitals, they are watching her, sniggering at her. She is one of them. She punishes her body by stuffing it, hitting it, she tries to exist outside of it, and she prays, *de profundis clamo ad te Domine*, she prays with all the fervour of her young heart that God will come to help her. *De profundis clamo ad te Domine. De profundis clamo ad te Domine. De profundis clamo, clamo, clamo ad te Domine. De profundis.*

She reads *Les Misérables*, and it isn't Cosette's childhood or Gavroche's death that upset her most, no. She sobs with gratitude all the way through the chapter where Victor Hugo explains how the sewers of Paris might be used to fertilise the countryside.

During long trips sitting in the back of the family car, she keeps her forehead glued to the window, her eyes staring into the distance, sinking down inside herself, somewhere in the depths where her thoughts disintegrate and escape her, where her daydreams have neither head nor tail, and while her parents are listening to Radio Classique in the front seat, and her brother and sisters are squabbling in the middle, she is gone.

On the weekends, she locks herself into her silent room at their country house, and reads. She reads everything, and lots of it. Sometimes, she extricates herself from her current book, feeling sore, her throat is sore, her jaw is sore, so sore she buries her head in her cushions, so she can shout, so she can vomit the great scream, so she can spit it out, so it gets out of her at last, she opens her mouth as wide as it will go, she exhausts herself, but nothing ever comes out, not a breath, not a sound, nothing. So then she swallows the pain, and takes up her reading again, feeling sick to her stomach. Page after page, she comforts herself, she forgets herself, she escapes herself.

She tries to be a good girl, not to disappoint. She feels sadder and sadder, she doesn't know why. She smiles, she lies, she pretends. She is ashamed. Above all, no-one must ever realise anything, no-one must ever guess, nothing must ever be noticeable.

SHE IS THIRTEEN, A boy snogs her at a party. She can't believe she is the one he chose, she does her best, to the point of getting an aching tongue and chapped lips, but it bores her. She writes him ardent messages that he never answers, she can't feel the mismatch between her burning words and her tense jaw.

She is very close to the sister who is three years older than her. Some nights, she helps her sneak out, she distracts their parents at the critical moment when her sister slips from the piano to the front door. She wakes up when her sister comes home, and rushes to nestle at the end of her bed and listen to stories about her night, about their tricks for getting into clubs when underage, about what everyone was wearing, about boys, about couples getting together, then breaking up, about the hesitations of the heart.

She takes drama classes and gradually develops a passion for the stage. She tells anyone who will listen that she's going to be an actress when she grows up. On stage, she allows herself to become a thousand faces, she doesn't need to pretend anything, she throws herself completely into someone else's arms, becomes incarnate. On stage, she tastes an intensity, a clarity of feeling she has never known anywhere else, and which might just be the warmth of life.

She doesn't collect words anymore. In her ancient Greek class, she learns how to take them apart, to follow their roots, which are entangled with the history of mankind.

One day, stunned, she understands "paedophile." Someone who is friendly towards a child. A sentence comes brutally back into her memory, like a slap in the face, an upside-down sentence, from the man in the stairwell.

I am your friend.

She would like to smash up her desk, burn the dictionaries, scream that words are liars, but this time, like so many other times, as soon as the fire rises, she puts it out. She is too frightened of these sudden rages to take the time to understand them, she smothers them as soon as they appear, then she rushes to the kitchen or the bakery to seal them away under soft bread.

She discovers that some words mean the opposite of what they claim to mean, but she doesn't yet wonder why these are precisely the words that are used.

*

During the Easter holidays, she goes with her family to visit the former East Germany. They spend a day at the Ravensbrück concentration camp and, as she reads the testimonies of the survivors, the reassuring illusion that evil and violence are specifically masculine traits comes tumbling down. Having learned only about men's wars from so many history books, she had naively protected herself from violence by considering it as exclusively male. At Ravensbrück, the tales of the cruelty and perversity of the female guards chill her to ice. Maybe it isn't Satan who keeps whispering dirty ideas to her, maybe it is she herself who is Satan.

Some days, sitting in silence on her bed with what seem like someone else's legs stretched out, she examines this body of hers with a sense of perplexity, she pinches it to check whether it can really hurt her. She does not recognise it.

And often, when her mind is on something else, she sees it, lying on the ground, dismantled, a few metres away from her. These invasive images don't affect her in any way, she doesn't question them, doesn't put them into words. She manages somehow.

In P.E. class, her body is a burden, she hates the taste of blood at the back of her throat when she runs, she hates her mottled red cheeks, she hates having her mind flooded with physical sensations that stop her from thinking. She hardly ever manages to catch a pass, when the ball is flying towards her she freezes. In dance class, she is absent from herself too often to be able to remember the choreography, so she slips to the back, where she can copy the others' movements without anyone noticing.

When the girls go to the stadium – I say the girls, it's a private Catholic middle school where the great majority of students are girls, and where the few boys have the status of demi-gods – so when the girls go to the stadium, at the edge of the Bois de Boulogne, often the same two or three flashers come to show their penises to the genteel young ladies.

On those days, she prays there won't be a long-distance race, that the teacher won't start the lesson with a few mumbled words, "Alright, O.K., so, when you get to the end of the track, you won't look, will you?" Because then, with every step that brings her closer to them, as she imagines their eyes upon her, she imagines, because she doesn't see them, because her own eyes are fixed on the ochre ground, and she feels dirty, so dirty, her red skin sizzles and exposes her to everyone, to them, as they smack their lips, around the first curve, she hasn't raised her head, it's hell just to keep breathing, she passes in front of them, she can feel their leering eyes hard hands moist penises, although they haven't moved, they are still there on the other side of the fence, she keeps running, she feels like she's in slow motion, like she has to tear her soles from the ground, another curve, she hates her buttocks wobbling so much, hates letting them see that wobble, and the further she moves away the better she can breathe, one more curve, then another, and then the whole thing starts all over again, passing in front of them again and again. Soon she doesn't feel a thing, and wonders how her legs manage to keep running without her.

IN *SECONDE*, SHE GOES out with an older man, a boy from *première*. They are alone at his place, he takes her into his parents' room, they lie down awkwardly on the bed, they kiss, they press together, they breathe each other, they are afraid, they are hot, they want it, he pulls down her pants, he touches her vulva. The moment he slides her pants down her thighs, she tenses up, something is broken, something disgusting spreads throughout her groin, her throat, the moment he touches her vulva she feels such a sudden hatred she could bash him to death. A second later, she is no longer there. He stops, flustered by her inert body. She apologises, gets dressed, and leaves. She breaks up with him over the phone the next day.

There's a new girl in her class, Sigrid. Purple Doc Martens and wicked sense of humour. Along with Marine, who has been held back a year, and whose father, as everyone knows, killed her mother with a shotgun when she was little and who is admired by everyone for her

31

witty repartee and insolence, they make a hell of a trio. They all belong to different friend groups, but they often escape to spend a few hours together, just the three of them, in a café, smoking cigarettes, setting the world to rights, sharpening their rebellious spirits, and laughing – laughing about everything – they understand each other so well, they loved each other immediately.

Marine never talks about her childhood, with its regular prison visits, or about the murderous father's return home a few months earlier. Marine is a bonfire of joy and intelligence.

Adélaïde doesn't say anything about the man in the stairwell, she never thinks about him, she lives a few metres further up, on the next floor, every day she is more joyful, more daring, she spins, she laughs, she can't keep still.

Sigrid confides that her older sister was raped and murdered by the East Paris Killer, five years earlier. She doesn't seek consolation, she is not waiting for answers, she mentions it once, just to be honest.

Marine, the sparkling one, dies two days after the end of the school year, of anorexia, alcohol, sleeping pills and sadness beyond repair.

*

Sigrid changes schools, they lose touch.

Years later, the National Automated D.N.A. Database, which Sigrid's father helped create, will transform my life.

I'll remember our unlikely trio, our daredevil desires, our tousled dreams, our pure, insatiable joys.

AT THE VERY END of the summer holidays, she is riding a moped, with her best friend hanging on the back, when a florist's van suddenly appears around the bend of the country road. Fractured skull, fractured wrist, brain injury, five missing front teeth, unresponsive body. Her friend is unscathed and distraught.

She goes into intensive care. In the ward, divided by drawn curtains, she can hear her neighbours without seeing them, and the hours tick past to the reassuring metronome of hearts beating together in the same hospital. One day, a few metres away from her, a heart goes haywire, footsteps hurry, the heart stops, the bed is moved away. And one night, she is the one who leaves.

No words can encompass the in-between-two-worlds which, for want of a better term, is called a near-death experience. I've sometimes tried to talk about it, but how do you describe something timeless, tender, infinite, inalienable, how do you put it into a sentence, how do you grasp it without crushing it, without shutting it away, without domesticating it. And so, yes, it was the happiest moment of my whole existence, and knowing that I'll return there is a great consolation on bitter days.

What drew me back to life that night was that I felt, so acutely that all my senses brimmed over, I felt, in my mouth and in my throat, the fireworks of an apple crunching in my teeth, I felt, in my nostrils and down my windpipe, the smell of pine needles rolling between my fingertips, I felt, in the palms of my hands, the moist, vibrant warmth of fistfuls of rich earth.

And then I fell into a thick sleep.

When she awakes, her body recovers its motor functions, without any possible explanation. When she awakes, she is afraid. Feeling like you're God, that's for crazy people. She barricades herself. What she caught a glimpse of, that night, is just not possible. So, now what? So, she's crazy. She seals up and locks away the loving light and the softness of infinity. When she awakes, she tells no-one about it.

Her condition stabilises, she is moved from intensive care to a room on the neurology ward. She'd like to see what she looks like, but her mother says she has left her powder compact at home, and the nurses point out that all the mirrors on the ward are screwed to the walls.

One night, she manages to slip out of bed, holding

on to her drips with shaking arms, she turns on the light in the bathroom. Someone is looking back at her from the mirror. Someone with a weird, swollen, blue face and a bloody mouth, a mouth that is now a gouged, gaping hole.

She says goodbye to her smile with a set of false teeth, which forces her, aged fifteen and a half, to stop sucking her thumb. Her mother had tried everything to get her to break that "big baby" habit: bitter nail polish, little bandages, and even a guinea-pig – a present contingent on a complete withdrawal. But the guinea-pig came to an early demise in the stomach of a country cat, and she started finding solace in her thumb again, ashamed and relieved to have this comfort within easy but now impossible reach.

Back in high school, she swaps her tight jeans and first pair of heels for floppy pullovers, wide trousers and lumberjack shirts she is constantly yanking down over her bottom. She pulls her strawberry blonde hair back in a tight bun.

Every time she passes a window or a mirror, she insults herself. When her mother and sisters take her shopping, she bursts into tears in the changing rooms. She'd like to look like them, but as soon as she tries on a pair of trousers, she can't do them up, they are always too tight around the bum, or else if she can do them up, they gape at the waist, even a belt won't fix it. Nothing fits.

She can't concentrate in class, she stares at the teachers' faces, her notes on the squared paper, her pen, she scribbles horrid faces in the margins, she fills in the silences, the blanks, she grips the tables, she resists, but every time the silent black wave crashes down on her without warning and she slips, absent, drifting between two tides.

One evening, some friends of her parents laugh at I can't remember what story, "Ah, Adélaïde, the alien of the family!" No-one has any idea how much this phrase affects her, how distant she feels from them all, and how much she wants to belong.

She spends the year crying in the school toilets, bingeing then vomiting, loathing herself, and, in public, showing off her false-teeth smile, doing well at school, playing the brave girl. That's the year she starts slapping herself, punching herself in the head, bashing the walls, constructing perfect suicide scenarios, suicides dressed up as accidents, unrecognisable suicides. She does not tell anyone about these ideas, these venomous jellyfish, she tries to isolate them inside an unintelligible, crude world, she convinces herself that there are these two distinct spaces, the vile treacherous body, and the pure, lively, joyous spirit.

*

At the end of *première*, the school offers the choice of a silent retreat at the Abbey of Bec-Hellouin or a visit to the châteaux of the Loire. Three days and two nights. She vaguely senses that she will not be able to keep control of herself in front of her friends for that long, so she is the only one to choose the silent retreat.

One night of infinite despair, crying *de profundis clamo ad te Domine* in a little empty chapel, someone sits next to her and slips an arm tenderly around her shoulders. The enormous white yeti, Jesus, whoever. Someone. Her sadness breaks like the dam of a reservoir lake in flood.

Until the next downpour.

AT A GIRLFRIEND'S COUNTRY house, there are three of them who often get together. One evening, the oldest one teaches the others how to pleasure themselves. She explains where the clitoris is, how you have to take it really gently, make tiny circles, not be shy about adding a little saliva, go slow, go fast, play with it. "I'll show you," she slips under a blanket and her hand going back and forth is visible under the folds, her fingers come back to her mouth for more saliva, her face flushes, she's breathless, her eyelids close, her attentive movements accelerate, she moans, she stiffens, her features tighten, she arches up. Silence. Her face is wide and relaxed. She opens her huge shining eyes and looks at her dumbstruck friends, smiling, her hair a mess, quite proud of herself.

Stupefaction. Other girls do this, it's not diabolical or shameful, it's normal? And so gentle!

She has a go, alone, trying to find the same innocence, the same confidence. She just can't. The caresses don't do anything for her, it's not strong enough, she needs violence. She decides her friend's way is useless, it doesn't work. Making it work has nothing to do with pleasure for her, it's about doing herself enough violence so she can leave her floppy body, go where she feels nothing, where she's suspended in mid-air, where she doesn't have to exist. So she can disgust herself, despise herself, hate herself.

She doesn't understand that these are two irreconcilable states, two opposite extremes that are covered by the same term, "masturbation". For her friends, a vibrant body, pleasure and excitement; for her, an absent body, contempt and inflammation.

In my family, bodily matters are not a topic of conversation, or, if they are spoken about, it's only to laugh at them. My father was nearly carried off recently by septicaemia, after treating it flippantly with his usual remedy: four big blankets, an aspirin and bed rest. In my family, complaining about little ailments lacks dignity. So, talking about sex? About that? About what she did when she was sure no-one could come in and no-one could see her, in the silence of her room, hiding in the undergrowth in the woods, perched up a tree, locked in the bathroom? About the terrifying and increasingly degrading scenarios she invented?

At high school, she manages to get her drama teacher to put on "Ondine" by Jean Giraudoux with her in the title role. As soon as she can, she goes for walks around the île aux Cygnes, under the pont Bir-Hakeim. There she becomes Ondine, the fish-woman, maybe a monster, but an enchanting, fantastic monster, and here is her kingdom, this furrow of land in the great river. She whispers long monologues to the weeping willows, she fills the eddies with Tritons, her long hair covers her breasts, and the madness of this desperate attempt to melt into someone else reveals its cruelty on opening night, when she freezes in the middle of a sentence in Act I. The prompt gives her the line, she doesn't respond, everyone hesitates, the lights go off, they think she has gone into the wings, the lights go on again, she hasn't moved, they start Act II rather bewildered, and suddenly, the crash of a body convulsing on the stage. She regains consciousness, stunned, in hospital. Her beautiful mermaid costume is sparkling forlornly on the hard bed. They explain that she has had an epileptic fit, that it is a frequent complication after a brain injury as serious as the one she had last year. She doesn't say anything but she knows very well, of course, what a *grand mal* is. She thinks that she has disobeyed, has wanted too much from life, and been punished.

She is seventeen, and going out with an older boy. He wants to make love, it's reassuring to think he knows how to do it, to make love, that he's already done it with others.

He has put clean sheets on the bed, lit a candle. She

gets undressed and sits at the edge of the bed. Naked, she feels cold. He lays her down, kisses her, asks her: "You O.K., I'm not hurting you?" She jumps, she had been absent. "Um, no, no it doesn't hurt." In truth she doesn't feel a thing, she's bored and doesn't know what to do with her hands.

They make love regularly, and every time, she is elsewhere. She tells herself that sex is all about doing boys a favour, it must be normal for girls not to feel anything. He is puzzled by her mute body, he asks questions, tries to find out what she likes. She doesn't know what to answer, doesn't want to disappoint him, says it's great, she loves it, and even, "It was cool when we did it on the floor."

She asks a friend for advice, the little noises, the expressions, the gestures she should try, she applies her lessons conscientiously, she mimes the pleasure and moans. She's passing the time. She avoids looking at or touching his penis. It's disgusting. All of that is of no interest to her. The senses, the flesh, it's all base, primitive. What she loves is literature and philosophy, she reads everything she can lay her hands on, she was awarded honours for her baccalaureate, and in two months she'll be going to the Hypokhâgne preparatory course for advanced literary studies.

They split up after the summer. He gets in touch regularly afterwards to ask her for news, and a couple of years later, asks "You still don't like it?" She retorts that no, she is above all that, that he's really obsessed. She won't be able to explain his sad and tender look, but she will think of it again, years later.

AT HYPOKHÂGNE, SHE MEASURES the extent of her vanity and ignorance by the length of the gigantic shelves in the library, where all the books are set texts, and by her marks in beginners' Latin: minus forty-five points out of twenty. She meets four wonderful women, who join her five faithful school friends in her heart.

Her mother takes her to see a different nutritionist. She is too plump, and steamed vegetables, grated carrots with lemon juice and 0 per cent-fat yoghurts do not seem to be making any difference. Once again, she says nothing about her eating frenzies, she doesn't count them, she refuses to accord them too much of an existence by putting them into words, she lies to others just as she lies to herself.

That year, she stops making herself vomit. When she pushes her fingers to the back of her throat, the anxiety this awakens is worse than whatever it is she is trying to calm.

She starts a new notebook with a sky blue cover,

a place to vent all her morbid thoughts, a collection of self-centred invective. She writes to tame the jellyfish, to stop herself from slapping herself in the face.

She spends the Easter holidays having a piece of bone from her skull grafted to her upper jaw, which has become necrotic at a staggering rate since the accident.

Her face swells up, you can hardly see her eyes or her nostrils. She looks like a hippopotamus that a Fauvist painter has embellished with yellow and purple patches. She loves looking at the hippopotamus in the mirror, her disfigurement has something extremely reassuring and sincere about it, with this face, she might be herself at last. But the graft doesn't take and her classical bourgeois features rise to the surface again.

She'd had a studious year until the bone graft, after which she takes the firm decision to become an actress. Since "Ondine", she hasn't set foot on a stage and she is itching to get back there. That fire, which illuminates her and lives inside her when she's performing, devours her when she's not on stage and, without the boards to contain it, consumes her.

She goes away for the whole summer to work as a counsellor at a girls' camp in Canada. For a few years now, she has spent a whole month in the heart of the Algonquin Park, exploring it from lake to lake, roasting marshmallows over log fires, and in the rustling of the pine needles and the calls of the loons, in the laughter and the singing, in all those nights spent gazing up at the Milky Way, she experiences sisterhood and confidence. Over there, the jellyfish keep still, she is wonderfully happy, affectionate and competent. Over there, there is no need for masks, everyone strives to give the best of themselves. Over there, the friendships she strikes up are for ever, over there, she is "Addy", an intense and luminous double, a great girl. She devours her days with the appetite for life of a prisoner out on leave, and at the end of each summer, she cries so hard on the return flight her jaws almost break.

This time, she gains nine kilos in two months. Her parents do not recognise her at the airport, their eyes slide over that flabby American in her hooded sweat-shirt, she has to wave her arms and call out, for them to finally see her in the crowd.

AT THE START OF the next academic year, she regis-
ters at the Sorbonne rather than going on to Khâgne,
the next level of her preparatory course, and she spends
two days a week studying at a conservatoire towards
the entrance examinations for the best drama schools.
She has only one word on her lips, "Theatre". The other
would-be actors seem to know everything about this
unfamiliar world, the great directors, the contemporary
playwrights everyone has read except her, the shows she
should not have missed, so she goes to plays almost every
night to catch up. She forms exalted friendships with
ardent young people from less privileged backgrounds,
who have come up to Paris to follow their dreams, to
make Theatre.

She is relieved to have found her path in life, because,
secretly, she had sometimes thought she might be
called to a religious vocation. And perhaps, between
the convent and the stage, between the saint and the

excommunicated actor, a desire vibrates. The same desire to serve, to surrender, to seek meaning outside of herself.

When I hear about priests raping children on the radio these days, I think about that frightened young woman, who hated herself so much that the unconditional love of God submerged her in gratitude, I think about her tears in churches, her desperate prayers, about those words, repeated thousands and thousands of times, *De profundis clamo ad te Domine*. Sometimes she wished she could devote her whole existence to Him, become clear water, day after day, confine her dirty body to a cell, her body with all those jellyfish that come and go inside her for which she knows no name other than "demons".

The priesthood, abstinence, religion, all these things are not a production line for child rapists, no, I don't believe that. But from the crowd of countless raped children, how many, once they were grown, chose the priesthood, abstinence, and religion as a safety barrier? God has no training in the psychological consequences of the trauma of sexual violence, God cannot stop dirty thoughts from erupting, I should know, I've prayed so much. And so, I think that among them, among those who sought refuge under vestments to feel less vile, there are some who give up fighting, some who devote themselves to hate, to unbridled power, and so yes, they use their profession with its built-in halo and the organised silence of their hierarchies to take their turn to rape and destroy with complete impunity.

She goes out with a young pharmacist for a few months. He is very much in love, very tender, he spends their nights together in endless cunnilingus trying to make her respond. She doesn't understand why he's exhausting himself. What a waste of time, what a bore sex is. She is nineteen.

For the first time, she tells him what she experienced that night after the accident, that in-between-two-worlds that she cannot explain to herself. A few days later, browsing for answers among the shelves in the science section of the Fnac bookstore, she comes across a book about near-death experiences. What? Others have experienced this, others have talked about it? Phew. She is not completely insane.

She starts reading all kinds of books about life after death, reincarnation, former lives, angels, prophecies, shamanism, altered states.

She learns how to roll joints and hold her liquor, she loves this fun, brazen girl who takes her place when she has been drinking.

One evening, she goes to see a play about the "love" of a mature woman for a very young boy and the misgivings of a judge who is upset at having to sentence her. The theatre is small and dusty, the audience is seated on benches, only a few steps away from the actress, and the further along the show progresses, the more she suffocates. She would like to stop everything, to shout, to sing at the top of her voice, to throw the benches over, but she can't even stand up to leave.

On the way home, she dashes off an account of that day in May when she was nine years old in her sky blue notebook. She calls it the "bad memory, the event, the ( )". She notes, "I am brutally catapulted into this little girl's body, so dissimilar to my present body. Everything is so precise, like a series of photographs, I remember it very precisely, but in a slightly external, strange way."

She does not know that some of the photographs are missing in her story, and that she will need years and years before she finds them intact again.

Shortly after that evening, she can no longer act. Whereas she used to be able to simply slip from one skin to another, she suddenly sees herself playing the actress, she thinks she's awful, so she piles it on, pretends, speaks too loudly or too quietly, keeps watch on herself, isolates herself.

The jellyfish are swarming now, they find their way through the spaces between her thoughts, and beneath their huge red umbrellas a thousand harpoons are charged with venomous words: I'm useless, I'm fat, I can't do this, I'm no good.

Sometimes, with no warning, when she's busy with something, when she hasn't seen a tight school of jellyfish forming around her, she suddenly feels sucked into the depths.

Her binges are more and more violent and more and more frequent, once or twice a day. In her sky blue notebook, she calls herself "a glutton, a greasy old bag, a sack of lard". She sees her body as full of pus. She imagines herself cutting away the extra flab with scissors, pushing the blades into herself, so it spurts out. She imagines it, but she doesn't do it, if she has scars or bandages she will be found out.

Her drama teacher thinks she hasn't found her voice, so she looks for singing lessons. Someone recommends an opera singer who dabbles in esoteric practices, who teaches bone conduction and vocal yoga.

Soon she cannot live without these sessions, where nothing comes out of her except raspy growls, smothered screams, sobs, and which she comes out of feeling unburdened and serene. She is convinced that she is on a spiritual path, and that all the suffering she is going through is a series of initiation tests, steps towards access to full consciousness. She reassures herself that, if anxiety is the flotsam left by previous lives, then she is not crazy.

She smokes cannabis more and more often. She fixes mini-spliffs in the evenings, which she puts into a metal box and starts smoking in the mornings as soon as she gets to university, before her first class. It allows her to forget, to let herself float, and her friends are less and less surprised by her absences.

She surrounds herself with comforting objects and rituals. She buys shoes that look kind, round and smiley, she weaves reassuring stories about them, like her "hyperspace rubbish-collector boots", green leather clunkers she wears almost every day, no matter what her incredulous girlfriends say. Year after year, she uses the same leather-bound, bible-paper diaries, piles of the same hardback notebooks with squared paper: navy blue covers for work notes, sky blue for her journal, red for her creative writing. She hardly ever writes in the red one.

In conversations, she makes her life sound more attractive, adds a bit of drama and suspense, improvises self-serving compromises with reality, backing them up with fake, racy anecdotes. Most of the time, they are fictitious, extremely detailed and completely pointless, and her girlfriends smile and forgive her for what they call "the enchanted world of Adélaïde". If people listen to her, she exists, and since everything always seems to slip away from her, she makes herself up.

Her room under the roof has a tiny makeshift balcony. She puts a chair next to the radiator and uses it as a stepladder, steps out of the window onto a cornice that rises gently up to a zinc-covered capstone shaped like a curly moustache. She goes up there to sunbathe, smoke cigarettes or joints, and write. On the blank days, the days when the jellyfish poison the horizon, she sits on top of the moustache in the stiff, precise pose of an old-fashioned automaton. There is a platform there, twenty centimetres square, her buttocks droop over the sides, and below her feet, the void. Up in mid-air on the seventh floor, she is swaying gently, terrifying and calm. All it would take would be for her to let herself slip over to one side, or fall forwards, to end it all.

SHE IS TWENTY YEARS old and often, when she needs to cross a street, she is hypnotised by the cars' ballet, by this body of hers waltzing from one vehicle to the next, then being dismembered beneath the black tyres. These images of herself cut into pieces have been with her for too long for them to frighten her, no, what terrifies her is that she might escape from her own vigilance and a jellyfish might drag her away for real, for ever, under the wheels, onto the tracks, out of the windows. And so she insults herself, slaps herself, bites her wrists. She waits by a wall for someone else to come along so she can fall into step beside them and get safely to the other side of the street. In the metro, she sticks to the wall on the platform. She doesn't go near the windows on the upper floors of buildings.

When she is with friends, she is joyful, she smiles, she is enthusiastic, she laughs out loud. If they knew, they would all run a mile. She has issues with compliments, she remains on guard, wonders what the person is after, what they want from her. If someone is sincere, she despises them. Are they blind or what?

She passes the entry exam for E.S.A.D., the École supérieure d'art dramatique, the Paris drama school. She gets in thanks to a scene where she was only standing in, reading lines for a friend, just to do her a favour, for the pure joy of acting. She drops her master's course at university, setting aside her planned dissertation on "The question of the monster in the myth of Ondine".

The day after the attack on the World Trade Center, she seeks refuge in the église Saint-Eustache. She has seen too many images, too much horror, she would like to stop those bodies falling endlessly in the blue sky behind her eyelids, so she lights a votive candle, gets down on her knees, cries and prays fervently for a long time, but something troubles her and forces her to the surface again, something, no, someone. Someone is looking at her. A man, thirty-ish, standing in the middle of the nave, his fly open, penis exposed. He stares at her, smiles, wanks.

The next day, she bravely goes back to the church, wanting to speak to the sacristan. He didn't see anything, but doesn't seem very surprised. He sighs, "You have no idea how many nutcases show up in churches."

A few days later, during a singing exercise, when she is tilting her rib cage back, she suddenly starts roaring, a long rasping sound that goes on and on and breaks into sobs, she is not screaming, she is vomiting rage, she is spitting out pain, she ends up panting and stunned on all fours on the Persian carpet. The teacher is at a loss. At the next class, she firmly suggests she go and get some help and gives her the number of a psychotherapist.

She doesn't call. She just can't.

At E.S.A.D., she is fascinated by everything she learns, she makes new friends, and a handsome guy, a student in the class above, kisses her one evening, whispering he'd been wanting to do that for a long time. Her heart sways with his tenderness, his sensitivity. He is in love, and little by little, his hands tame her, reassure her. He reads *The Art of Love* to her, he imagines her running in airy white cotton dresses through fields of ripe wheat, she is not always sure if she is the girl in his imagination, but no matter, he is so handsome, so gentle.

One evening when she has smoked enough weed to be able to offer him her thighs, and he slips his tongue between them, she lets herself be carried away for the first time by the strong, soft waves, she arches her back unthinkingly, her breath is short and her cheeks flushed, her brain is bewildered, her body shudders, moans, radiates, her hands are alive and occupied, she wants him so intensely. The words desire and orgasm will no longer be empty words for her, but they will remain rare words.

*

The better life goes for her, the more she feels out of her depth. The schools of jellyfish surge up without giving her the time to get out of sight, she breaks down in class, in the street, in the arms of her lover. Her joys have dark blue circles of solitude beneath them. She stops telling herself that this is just her emotional chakras opening, that it will pass, that she's coping. She is always changing personalities, she's afraid of being psychotic, schizophrenic, bipolar, raving mad. She is afraid she will never dare to say anything to a therapist. She is afraid of being committed if she ever does tell all. She is afraid there's nothing wrong with her at all, that she is lying to herself and keeping her own head under water to escape her own crass mediocrity, her conformism.

She would like to talk to her parents about it, but she can't find a way. She plays the role of the great girl with the bright smile perfectly, and they explain her crumpled face on bleak mornings as the intractable moods of a budding artist. She suffers from her forced isolation and her lack of sincerity with her family, but she doesn't know how to cross the ocean of her held-back tears. She is exhausted from carrying herself, from pulling herself into her body every morning, that body drooping over her bed like clothes on a hanger, from hauling herself to the end of each day and going to sleep at night, with the anxiety of time passing, so quickly, without waiting for her to catch up.

SHE CALLS THE PSYCHOTHERAPIST the day after
she turns twenty-one. He has no availability for new
patients, but she apologises so profusely that he suggests
she come see him anyway, just for one session.

To get to his practice, a code, a heavy metal door, a
long cobblestoned walkway, and suddenly a serene,
lush courtyard, with a big Chartreux cat who comes to
meow between her calves. The room is on the ground
floor, you go in with no ceremony, no preliminaries. It's
a small space with egg cartons stuck all over the walls, a
fastidious addition by a cellist seeking good acoustics.
A sofa bed, a few cushions, a box of tissues, a wicker
wastepaper basket. And a chair, facing her, where a
benevolent man is sitting, looking at her.

As soon as she sits down, she starts crying, she cries
for an hour without being able to say a word. The next
day, she sends him a postcard of an Egyptian statue
whose face is ravaged by chisel marks. On the back, she
simply writes, "Thank you".

*

He refers her to a young therapist, a woman with a bulging belly, haloed by the radiant certainty that sometimes comes in pregnancy. The sessions take place in a long room looking out onto the street, a rectangle of beige carpet surrounded by cheap mattresses and faded cushions, dimly lit by a row of windows with frosted glass. The door opens out onto a permanently dirty pavement.

This woman works with "transgenerational" issues, the unconscious heritage of unresolved grief and trauma from our dear ancestors, and so, for the next session, she has to draw up a family tree from memory, and add any family events that seem important to her.

She does this conscientiously and doesn't see anything very interesting there, until the therapist underlines thirteen instances of words like "accident, run over, defenestration." In all those lives, the only things she had remembered were the accidents, the illnesses, the suicides. In her own short life, nine accidents, and "sexual contact".

She quickly dismisses this episode. "I was lucky, it was just unwanted sexual contact, and my parents took it well, they realised something was wrong, they didn't ask any questions, they just called the police. I don't think that's what my problem is, I never even think about it. What I feel, right now, when I think about it? Well . . . I don't feel anything in particular, it doesn't bother me in any way. And anyway, when it happened, I didn't even cry in the police car, I remember smiling when they put the flashing lights on."

"You set up a pattern of resistance to deal with challenges, you'll have to work on that one day."

With her girlfriends, she is always radiant, and while she sometimes confides in them, she never offers more than a few light words, she doesn't dwell on it, no, she runs, she scatters herself, she heads in a thousand directions every day. The more despairing and dark she feels in her inner depths, the brighter she shines on the outside. A will-o'-the-wisp.

For a few months now, she's had a strange cough, a cork in her throat that her daily vocal exercises can't pop. With her family and boyfriend, she has the high, irritating voice of a little girl, and on stage her voice thickens, deepens, softens. This annoys her, she can tell that neither of these voices belongs to her, and she has no idea where hers might be.

One evening, after smoking a joint, she draws the two postures her body usually assumes, in her navy blue notebook. She has noticed that she has almost always been like this, whether standing up, sitting down, at home, at school, on public transport. Then, in a long paragraph, she analyses how these positions certainly obey to an "intuitive rebalancing of energy".

The two stiff figures have neither heads nor feet. In one of them, the arms are stuck to the bust, the left hand, making a fist, hides the pubis, the right hand grasps the left. In the other figure, one arm is wrapped around the lower abdomen, the other one squashes her breasts. Constrained body, shameful body, hated body.

At the end of this first year at drama school, a teacher lashes out, saying her acting is off-key, too much outside of herself, another one says she needs to "go down into her vagina". In her notebook, despairing at these comments, she asks herself, "How do you go down into your vagina?"

She starts the summer with a second bone graft from her skull to her jaw, which takes hold this time, but from which she awakes feeling bled dry. She doesn't take pleasure in anything that summer, especially not herself. She stuffs herself to forget, to drown in the deep folds of her own flab, to become a useless jelly-like mass, a great big jellyfish beached on a rock. She dumps the tender and attentive boyfriend, their hideous love disgusts her.

A summer spent hating herself so much, thinking so constantly about suicide, that she decides, when evening comes and she has no strength left in her, to talk to her worried parents. She puts a little of her solitude, her inadequacy, her suffering into words. She hides the hatred, the violence, the psychotherapy. They listen to her without judgment, they console her and take her tenderly in their arms. It has been so long since they have allowed themselves to do that.

When the academic year starts, the psychotherapist has moved to a distant suburb, and writes to her several times to "strongly advise" her to go to a therapy group (three hours every Thursday evening) in the same long room looking out onto the dirty street, led by the first therapist she saw. That "above all she mustn't stop now she is on the right track". That she is "worried by her silence".

The idea of having to talk to despairing strangers about her desperate stories holds no particular attraction, so she doesn't answer her letters or telephone calls.

She has lots of short flings that last an evening or two, and her friends diagnose her as suffering from an advanced stage of Batman/Joker syndrome. Every time she meets a guy, he's The One, the father of her future children, the eighth wonder of the world, and all it takes is some small thing, a body odour, an awkward gesture, a tender word, for Batman to fall down a trapdoor and for the Joker to appear. Suddenly she turns from the wonder-struck, sensuous girl into an icy wooden log. Luckily, she doesn't sleep with all the Batmen she meets, many of them will never know what went on between the two of them behind the curtains of her closed eyelids. She is playing for high stakes, falling for anyone who will have her, like the young painter-decorator who locks her up at his place, and who is so violent she only gets away from him *in extremis*, under a volley of abuse.

At drama school, the singing teacher tells her she is blocking her voice at the back, that she is not letting it vibrate, that she is not giving anything of herself. He tells her about the fog that the sound can't get through, and so, during every lesson, she bravely searches for her vocal cords, but she never manages to feel them, to find them. It's enough to make her want to bang her head against a wall, as if the whole front of her throat had been wiped away.

A few days before Christmas, another dental surgery, another spell of feeling blank and beaten up. She resolves to go to the group therapy sessions.

In her sky blue notebook: "Puzzled after last night, it seems to me that my neuroses are of another order than a simplistic explanation of the responsibilities of parents. And anyway, do we actually need to understand and explain it all? Everything is beyond us."

The following week: "Wonderful session last night. Three hours of sobbing, jolts to my body, internal earthquake. This morning, I got up feeling light as a feather!"

And the next one: "Now I'm lost in the depths of my being again, I don't know anything anymore, it's as if

I'm awash with endorphins, I've felt dreadfully calm these last few days. Who is whispering behind me? What defence is this? What elephants' graveyard, what monsters will I have to confront? For which princesses?"

IN THE SPRINGTIME, SHE is twenty-two years
old and still singing the same old tune of suffering and
solitude. She slaps herself in secret because she can't
cut her skin. In summer, her body is exposed, her mother
would see the marks. In company, she smokes cigarettes
to keep her hands busy, smokes hash to stop herself
from thinking, and drinks to cheer herself up. She
discovers M.D.M.A., ecstasy, hallucinogenic mushrooms
and all those incredibly funny and loving girls she
becomes when she is no longer herself.

She spends the group therapy sessions crying, never man-
aging to put her tears into words. When the therapist
offers to see her for individual sessions, she is relieved
to return to the pretty courtyard, with the cat between
her legs and the funny room lined with egg cartons.

In another operation before the summer, the surgeon
opens up her jaw, which is not even a year old, to put in
three implants. In the chrome of the examination light,

she sees her open jaw, and the surgeon's busy hands inside. She looks at herself without recognising herself, that hole is not her mouth.

She spends the summer swimming, melting into the wide blue expanse of sea, letting herself be carried by the waves, listening underwater to the crystal echo of the world, feeling her long hair spread and dance around her.

One evening, she writes in her sky blue notebook, after deeply gashing her foot: "Looking at them lined up, the string of stupid accidents I've had over the course of my short life, could swallow me up like a boa constrictor. Always the same symptoms repeating themselves, accidents, obsessive thoughts about death, general fatigue, endless self-criticism, lack of a distinct identity, bipolar, doubts, lack of love. And I still don't understand it all, except that they will never stop until I do understand it all. But what the fuck is there to understand? I'm exhausting myself running on a carpet that just keeps rolling itself up."

Autumn comes, and in her navy blue notebook, she notes:

Resolutions for the new school year:
– stop pushing my neck forwards when I act
– voice from the throat

- no more overacting
- get rid of the plaster Angel Gabriel face (why am I
  so afraid of living?)

Before Christmas, another operation. They are going to
open up the gums around the implants, stick another
scalpel into the flesh, which has barely formed scars
from the previous scalpel, poke the needle in and pull
it out again, yank on the thread. She shivers all through
the night before the operation, she can no longer stand
her foreign, numb mouth after the anaesthetic, and
those hands inside it, cutting, banging, sewing.

A month goes by before she can surface for air.

At E.S.A.D., she works hard, she makes progress, the
teachers keep an attentive eye on her: "Where are your
legs, go down into your body, Adélaïde! Come down
from the control tower!"

The dance teacher introduces the students to the
Feldenkrais Method. Lying on the ground, they have to
make tiny movements, welcoming and carefully exploring all of their physical sensations. How the right leg
responds to the left arm, how the knee has a thousand
unknown ways of bending, how the feet can make the
head nod.

She finds it all very difficult, and absolutely new. Her
body, that sticky old pile of dying cells, her own body,

a wild and unknown continent? She initiates the first negotiations of the peace process.

When the stomach cramps and the knot in her throat appears, she breathes, she concentrates, she plays for time. First, get away from people, anywhere as long as she can't be seen, bedrooms, kitchens, churches, entryways, corners. Then, curled up, let the jellyfish slide into her, and howl, without making a noise, her hands over her gaping mouth, rocking, looking for a nice dirty image to immobilise herself, to calm herself down. Still lurching, get up, splash some water on her face, too bad if it's holy water, massage her jaw, open her eyes wide, pinch her cheeks, tidy her hair, and off she goes again.

In the street, in bars, at parties, she is always the security guard on duty, she starts, she stares, she stakes out, she listens. That guy over there with the shifty eyes. That other one who never turns round and she can't figure out from the back. All of them are suspicious. Her friends complain that she's only half-listening to what they say, that she never remembers their stories, and it's true, often she only hears the last few words, so she can ask a new question, and then she won't listen to the answer, because she's too absorbed, keeping watch.

When she's had nothing to eat, she is incapable of feeling carefree. When she's drunk or on drugs, she rushes to seduce anyone who makes her feel uneasy, she plays at the edge of the abyss, she is calmer when she is afraid.

The jellyfish swarm on the mornings after her benders. One Sunday, out on the cornice, she moves forwards, she's about to fall, one step more, and then . . . almost nothing, a breath of wind, she shivers, she moves back. After that Sunday, she is wary of hard drugs, she forces herself to only take them exceptionally, and only on the condition that she will not be alone the next day.

She spends time at some friends' squat. That's where they rehearse, perform, have fabulous parties. She identifies the frightening strangers and, as soon as she's had something to drink, she comes on to them, like that guy leaning on the counter, ogling her like a butcher assessing a carcass. With the fake air of carelessness that she loathes and yet mechanically adopts in these situations, she goes up to him, starts a conversation, and he stares at her, touches her, gropes her. Worse luck, he's a regular, she sees him again at every single party, and each time, without being able to explain it to herself, she forces herself to say hello, to submit again and again to his dirty looks and his wandering hands. She always manages to escape in time, but she doesn't sleep well, she has troubled dreams, where she is all alone, he sees her, he comes near, he smiles, he takes out his penis. She wakes up with a start, her body feeling tense with pleasure and hatred.

She decides she can't go to parties anymore.

She obstinately searches for an explanation for the jelly-fish. Some days, she tells herself it's the accident when she was fifteen, which took her from a carefree, happy life to being conscious of its finitude. On others, it's the hurdles inherent to a pathway of initiation to full consciousness. Or the limitations of bourgeois life, and the terrifying vacuity of social masks. In her family, there are certainly a few unacknowledged skeletons and several locked and bolted closets. She keeps looking. She goes to all the group sessions, all her individual sessions, all the yoga and voice sessions. She stops buying cannabis. She wants to understand, she wants to move forwards. Her passion for life roars and throws her into a terrifying rage that she finds difficult to hide under the ice of politeness.

In individual therapy sessions, she often stumbles against the same threshold: she is sad and discouraged, she concentrates, she breathes, she takes her awareness down into her body, and anger suddenly burns her throat, her mouth distends itself without a single word coming out, she's suffocating and then, very quickly, she is no longer there, no longer sitting in the room wallpapered with egg cartons, but little and lost and frozen, standing in an immense white desert, waiting.

She calls this place "my little girl on the ice floe", she has no idea that this little girl still has a long wait for me.

SHE IS TWENTY-THREE. She starts writing the story of *Jeanne, With the Plaster-Coloured Eyes*. She thinks about it a lot, she doesn't write much.

She plays a small part in a popular crime series and one day, after a very early start, she is resting in a trailer, curled up in one of the comfortable make-up chairs. One of the main actors comes in, she pretends to be asleep. She doesn't like the way he's been staring at her, his constant comments about her buttocks, how he calls her "his white Negress". He comes closer, she doesn't move, she keeps her eyes shut and suddenly, a pair of thick lips are on hers. She is petrified, he bursts into a great loud laugh and leaves without saying a word.

In the springtime, she falls madly in love with a super-talented guitarist with aniseed-green eyes, they are both equally awkward and emotional, she spends almost all her nights at his place.

They make love, but every time he penetrates her, he has to force himself in and she has to grit her teeth, her tight vagina is always dry. Once he is inside her, she learns how to relax and sometimes discovers the dizzying delight of simultaneous orgasms. Just as long as he doesn't put his fingers anywhere near her thighs. Just as long as she is drunk enough, if what he wants is a blowjob.

She is coming to the end of her three years at E.S.A.D., and the day after the public presentations she wakes up feeling nauseated. The compliments she received as she came off the stage, "stunning, beautiful, radiant", make her want to throw up. She doesn't know that girl they are talking about.

On the occasion of a wedding, she goes back to the scene of her moped accident, eight years previously. Nothing of what she has experienced since then has had the enveloping beauty of that night at the border post of her existence, so she hangs on to the sensations that pulled her back to life that night – the fireworks of an apple crunching in her teeth, the smell of pine needles rolling between her fingertips, the moist, vibrant warmth of fistfuls of rich earth – she hangs on so she doesn't slip off a roof or fall out of a window.

In the autumn, she swaps her vocal yoga class for Feldenkrais Method classes, which she discovered the previous year.

One day, the teacher is absent and someone else is replacing her. She observes the bodies lying flat on the ground with the tender attention of an entomologist towards unknown insects. She looks at Adélaïde working, suggests a few movements and asks her:

"Tell me, when I ask you to align your pelvis with the rest of your body, how do you do that?"

"I check it with the floorboards, or against my arms beside my body."

"O.K., so in fact, you use the floor, or your arms, to find out what position your pelvis is in?"

"Yes, that's right. Is that not what I'm supposed to do?"

"You're starting on the outside to understand an internal movement. Could you try it the other way round? Try to feel your pelvis from the inside and adjust your position accordingly?"

For the rest of the session she tries and tries, but no matter how hard she tries, she just can't find a way to inhabit her pelvis. She can feel her feet, her calves, her thighs, then her abdomen, her chest, her arms, her skull. In the centre, a hiatus, a hollow, where sensation gets swallowed up only to reappear somewhere else.

This stops her from sleeping that night, and she remembers all her drama teachers' comments, her lovers' uncertainties, the boredom she feels when she must make love. She can't feel her pelvis! She's been living with a fake, a facsimile that nothing innervates.

Her real pelvis has disappeared. A long time ago, no doubt, since she had no idea that it could be any different. She doesn't understand.

During the daytime, she takes driving lessons and goes to one audition after another; in the evenings she vibrates with the effervescence of the young jazz scene at the concerts her sweetheart takes her to. She needs to be distracted from herself.

Just after Christmas, more than two hundred thousand people die in the tsunami that ravages the Indian Ocean. She feeds on the photos of the blue, swollen corpses haunting the newspapers. She hates herself for doing so.

A director from the May 1968 generation, with a lively and equally meandering intelligence, hires her for his next creation. She has already been cast in a few television films, but this is the first time she will be acting on stage with professionals, and she is punch-drunk. The actor playing the love interest explains that they will have to "go out for coffee, have a drink or two, get to know each other, to strengthen their chemistry on stage". She believes him, he's more experienced than she is. And he seems nice enough.

Even at their first coffee, at place Denfert-Rochereau, he flirts, she's embarrassed, she feels obliged to let slip,

"I'm sorry, I have a partner."

He answers with a cheeky smile, "What do you think is going on here?" She feels vaguely guilty about the forced intimacy he is trying to set up.

The cast and crew are friendly and welcoming, she wants to fit in. Everybody smiles at their obvious complicity, finds them cute, the pair of them, but his words feel sticky and revolting, she hears them even when he isn't around. His hands wander, brush against her, a little more precisely every day. She has violent stomach cramps, she sobs in the metro without knowing why, she has disgusting nightmares.

When the performances begin, he forces himself on her and kisses her behind the curtain, just before she goes on stage. When they are on stage, in the dark, and the audience's attention is elsewhere, his hands wander over the small of her back and grab her buttocks, and she can't move to get away from him.

One night, he nearly kills her in his car. He wanted to take her home, he was alarmingly drunk, he was so insistent she didn't dare refuse. He spent the whole trip playing the whining lover jilted by the frigid bitch, and she clutched her seat at each turn of the steering wheel. The car ended up on the pavement, between a bench and a plane tree.

She doesn't say anything to her boyfriend, or to her therapist, or to anyone. She believes him when he tells her she is "stuck-up, cold, insensitive", when he

insinuates that it's her fault, that she is the one torment-
ing him, provoking him. The jellyfish established their
empire inside her too long ago for her to discern
these new tentacles. Her stomach aches, she loses her
voice, she becomes anxious before going on stage, but
she doesn't see the connection, she just thinks she's
complicated.

She goes to see a voice specialist after losing her
voice for the umpteenth time: "Functional dysphonia
with tension +++ in the jaw." She is prescribed a series
of exercises to do twice a day. She can never make it
to the end of the series, as soon as she starts moving
her jaw the jellyfish loom: breaking her forehead open
and making blood run down her face, raining lashes all
over her body, widening her smile with a pair of scissors.
The voice specialist says she is not taking the exercises
seriously enough, but how can she explain? She cancels
all her future appointments.

After the play, she fails all her auditions: too outside
herself, too wound up, too keen, too tense. She writes
in her sky blue notebook: "How do you believe in yourself, when you are so alone? The future is a blank slate
where I am afraid of slipping."

It will take almost ten years for me to apply the terms
"sexual harassment" and "sexual assault" to that actor's
behaviour, to that forced kiss from the star of the

television series, ten years to come to terms with the disaster that those first professional experiences were for me, ten years to stop feeling guilty.

AT TWENTY-FOUR, SHE KEEPS running round like a headless chicken, pursuing a thousand activities, stuffing her mind with projects. At night, she dreams she is running late, during the daytime, she manages never to be early. Never to leave any room for the jellyfish.

If a man's gaze slides over her without stopping, she's no longer quite sure of her existence. So she laughs, shakes her hair, clowns about, talks all kinds of nonsense just to be interesting, just to see herself reflected in the pupils of the eyes across from her, to prolong the fugitive sensation of belonging to the living, of being part of the common, intelligible, ordered world.

Her therapist talks to her about Family Constellations, he thinks this method might help her discover what the "little girl on the ice floe" is waiting for. She signs up for a weekend workshop.

It's at the same place as the group therapy sessions, there are about ten of them there, sitting on mattresses.

After a round of names and how everyone is feeling, the first constellation starts. The therapists ask two or three succinct questions of the young man who volunteered to be the seeker, and invite him to choose representatives of his parents and grandparents from the other participants. Then the representatives move around on the beige carpet, finding the place that feels right for them, attentive to the sensations and images that appear within and between them. Little by little, step by step, under the astonished eyes of the silent seeker, an old family story emerges from the void. It's exciting, there are incredible twists, stunning discoveries, intense emotions.

She raises her hand to be next, she is so keen to discover at last what has been terrifying her. But the person who incarnates "what the little girl on the ice floe is waiting for" terrifies the representatives of the family, without anyone being able to name it, without anyone seeming to know what it is. The therapists console her, "Constellations only reveal what the seeker is capable of discovering. The information will come when you are ready to receive it."

She comes away from the weekend with a sense of relief. She has found a way to make sense of her story.

That summer she goes to Italy to train with a woman director who is a disciple of Jerzy Grotowski. Everyone works their body and voice to the point of exhaustion, to the point where they cannot take anything anymore, do not want anything anymore, and, at last, something new and alive happens. No matter how hard she struggles, the exhaustion doesn't make her relax, she never lets down her guard. She can't feel the difference between dramatic tension and muscular tension. When she makes an effort to relax her face, the vice in her throat tightens even more, stifling her feelings and slurring her speech. She feels stuck inside herself.

She later takes a second, then a third training course in the juicy splendour of the Tuscan countryside, with its figs and valleys, trying to tear away, with her bare hands, all the obstacles she so patiently wrought to protect herself from the jellyfish.

She goes away for a few days to a family house, with the firm intention of making progress in writing *Jeanne*. She writes very little, sleeps, stuffs herself and masturbates with brutal contempt.

Afterwards, when her boyfriend remarks on a train that she has put on more weight, she slaps him.

That year she is struggling to reach the minimum number of hours she needs to be eligible for her actors' temporary-status employment benefit, so she does some voiceovers for an American porn show. Young cameramen go to student drinking parties and coerce the girls who have drunk the most. In exchange for a T-shirt or a cap, they start by showing their breasts to the camera and end up masturbating, alone or with their girlfriends, in a tour bus turned into a studio. She has to imitate them saying "Oh" and "Ah", turn their "My God Oh Ah Oh my God Yes" into French. She inventories hundreds of images of their pink vulvas, their brown vulvas, their hairless, marketed vulvas, which appear detached from those young women's bodies, who are themselves formatted, all alike, letting out the same cries in the same postures, conforming to what the cameraman wants them to do, ignoring their own sensuality, their wildness, their romanticism, thinking they are liberated when they are being exploited.

She is neither appalled nor shocked, she is just like them, their contradictory desires are the same colour as her own swamplands.

She notes down a New Year's resolution: "Take my fears by the hand and face the Barbarian."

And a little while later: "I am so sad, if only I could figure out why."

The nights she sleeps alone, she often has the same nightmare. She is standing in darkness, she smells a strange smell, soft and revolting, little by little her eyes get used to the darkness and she can make out the uneven, moving walls of a small room. Four blind walls, a floor, a ceiling. The walls are covered with scarlet muscles, lined with flesh, they pulse. *Ba-boom ba-boom*, she knows this rhythm, *ba-boom ba-boom*, she has this rhythm on the tip of her tongue, *ba-boom ba-boom*, what it is now? It's her heart lying there, in her hands, her bony white hands, it's her flesh, her own flesh, which makes up these walls, and this wasted skeleton standing in the middle of the room, that's her too, and the skeleton starts to bounce, to rebound, it bangs against the walls and its sharp bones tear off long ribbons of blood, white viscous jets come together and congeal, the room gets smaller and smaller, and the more blood and fat there is, the less air there is, the more she suffocates. She pulls herself out of sleep, half-drowned.

In therapy she explores a few issues that bring her peace for a time, then end up being dead ends. Her bingeing, sadness and brutality never disappear for very long, a few days maybe, sometimes a week or two. She lives on a dotted line. The more she scratches at the varnish of closed doors, or ransacks the attics, or beats the under-growth, the more she resents her sisters, her brother, her parents, her grandparents, and all of her ancestors.

She takes part in four more Family Constellation weekends, she tries Holotropic Breathwork, rebirthing, primal scream therapy, kinesiology, floral remedies, St John's wort, she sees an etiopath, an astrologer. She reads a pile of books on personal development, on

Indian spirituality, on Nonviolent Communication, she discovers Jung and Schopenhauer. She's like those crazy birthday candles that keep lighting up again and again until you drown them in a glass of water, she is the grand-daughter of a legionnaire and, as long as there's a war on, she goes to the front.

SHE IS TWENTY-FIVE AND sees her days stretching, spreading, unfolding ahead of today just as they did behind yesterday, with always the same sticky red smear as she drags her body along.

She persists in trying to write the story of Jeanne. Sometimes, just as soon as she starts a scene, she stumbles on a word. She picks it up, meticulously examines each of its facets, crumples and smooths out phrases and syntax, but the words always have a meaning hiding behind hers, there is always one that she hasn't opened up and whose contents overwhelm her and take her away, a vowel that rings a little too clear, non-consensual rhymes, random felicities. She gets lost within a few sentences. Sometimes she stops writing without realising it, she slips and sinks, with all the weight of her old body, into the dark waters. Afterwards, she shakes herself dry, she goes to the bathroom to splash cold water on her face, standing in front of the mirror for a long time without seeing herself. Only a few more hours before the end of the day.

*

At auditions, she is a caricature of herself, she blushes, she stutters, she crushes herself under her own feet. She can't make any plans beyond the day after tomorrow, she is incapable of making the simplest telephone call, of taking care of any administrative matters. She is over the top and down in the dumps, she is upside down and back to front.

And so, after one of her many failed auditions, when someone tells her about an acting coach, she signs up for a three-day course.

There are a dozen or so participants, in loose clothing and bare feet, all equally kind-hearted and hungering for an existence. After a careful and gentle warm-up of each part of the body, they spread out around the room, and, as soon as everyone is ready, a song starts up. The instructions are to let the body be free to express what is happening to it, here, right now, to be filled with this voice, these lyrics, this music. She dances, she jumps, she is elated, she whirls round, she falls to the floor, she starts again, she expends incredible energy, she is happy, but very quickly the teacher points out, "You are telling yourself pretty stories. You pretend to be moved but in reality you're making it all up, you're not showing anything, you won't let yourself be touched. When someone obstinately wants to hide a part of them-selves, nothing of their self filters through except their obstinacy to hide themselves." Hit and sunk. At last, a safe haven where she can lay down her weapons and learn how to act again. Here is someone who won't let her bluff, won't allow her to cheat.

She ends up staying three years at the École du Jeu. Time enough to dismantle her battlements brick by brick, to uncover herself, to want too much, to despair, to give up, to start again, to work, to give herself up at last. Time enough to no longer recognise herself. Time enough to get to know herself.

Night after night, her wonderful love life with her darling guitarist unravels. She feels so alone. They still love each other just as much, but neither of them can decipher the other's silences anymore, each too absorbed by their own emptiness. She can't seem to find the desire she felt at the start, more often than not she just lets him penetrate her, since he seems to want to, since she owes him that at least, since they are a couple.

With her girlfriends, she hangs on to her smile like a casta-way to a raft, and being like everyone else for a few hours floods her with wild joy every time. Outside her circle of close friends, people think she is hysterical, always "doing an Adélaïde", exclaiming, laughing too loud, bursting into flame too quickly, and it's true that in public she can't sit still, she whirls, she pirouettes, she jumps, always making sure she never stands too long on the same board.

Two days a week at the *École du Jeu*, she works at undoing her habits, not using tricks, paying attention to what feels right within herself. She tinkers with her locks: her frigging pelvis that gets stuck for no reason, the knot in her throat that darkens her voice, the forlorn smile that gags her lips. Some days her jaws hurt so badly that she can't even chew, so she drags her friends to the Indian restaurant where she can swallow a dhal, or she discreetly cuts her food into tiny pieces.

The rest of the week, she works here, there and everywhere. Some evenings, she wishes she could just leave it all behind, just walk straight ahead without stopping until she falls asleep like a log. A man would be there when she wakes up, and he would say, "Get up and walk", with his finger pointing in a particular direction, and she would get up, she would know where to go at last. Or she could just bury herself in the ground and rot with the autumn leaves.

Around Christmas, she goes backpacking in Southern India with her boyfriend.

In Thanjavur, they go to the Brihadishvara Temple. It is very early, the huge ochre granite edifice vibrates in the red sky, the crowds of tourists, worshippers and beggars are not yet swarming, they are almost alone. Something inside her releases, or relaxes, her heels press

87

into the ground as her body rises up, her steps become heavier, as heavy as the eighty-tonne stone at the summit of the sanctuary, the keystone of the sky all around. They pass countless statues of Shiva dancing in the first soft rays of morning sunshine. They take off their sandals and step into the sanctuary, to attend puja. This ritual has not meant very much to her until now, but this morning she is shivering. They wait a long, long time, sitting a few metres away from the moiré curtain which hides the divinity, and all they can hear from whatever is happening on the other side are clatters, rustling and hushed voices. At last the curtain is drawn back: a gigantic black stone lingam, standing on a large yoni. The bare-chested Brahmins are perched on a balcony to reach it, they shower it from great bowls held at arm's length, with clear water, white milk, melted butter, all of these liquids running down the grooves of the enormous wet stone, mixing and flowing into the yoni. The curtain falls.

She remains sitting there, dumbstruck. She can't get over what she has just seen: two enormous sexual organs, the erection of the one streaming with sperm inside the other, or a new-born baby glistening with amniotic fluid spurting from the womb, Creation, Beauty itself, absolute, intimate, raw. At that moment she belongs to something immense that she doesn't know how to define.

She visits the rest of the temple in silence, full of excitement and desire, keenly aware of the delicate little statues in their acrobatic poses, intertwined and grasping each other, grabbing and caressing hips, their breasts and penises erect, tongues busy, for all eternity.

In her own churches, statues only swoon in pain or affliction, and when there are naked women at the top of columns, they have little devils poking forks into their buttocks. In her language, sometimes you make love, but more often than not, men subjugate, take, possess, penetrate, shaft, screw, pummel and tear women apart. They make a mess of them, they shoot their load. In her country, the icy presentations of fashionable magazines eroticise pain and humiliation, and when liberated women are shown enjoying their unbridled sexuality, they are generally tied to the bedposts talking up how good it is for their skin to have sperm sprayed all over their faces.

That day she realises that she knows nothing of her sexuality except a poor frightened and confused ghost, disfigured by shame, eaten up with guilt, while others celebrate the Joy of being in the world by embracing each other's bodies.

SHE IS NEARLY TWENTY-SIX years old, she would like to spend less time thinking about the circumference of her arse and the crass mediocrity of her little person. She needs someone to take her in their arms so badly, and it's so difficult to ask.

At the *École du Jeu*, she stumbles in the same net, day after day, the one she set to protect herself from the jellyfish. She tries to feel something that she hasn't imagined or invented, any kind of basic emotion, but as soon as she gets too close to herself, she freezes and absents herself, so she steps back, goes around it, pretends.

One afternoon like many others, with no clue or warning, she is working on feeling her pelvis to music and the jellyfish rise up, swarm all around her, crush her, stuff their tentacles into her mouth, she can't breathe anymore, she is suffocating, she falls to the ground, the ground falls away beneath her, she panics, she is going to die of fright, to die for real. The teacher grabs hold of her, "Look at me! Look at me, Adélaïde, come back to us, stop telling yourself stories, it's not real!" She desperately hangs on to those eyes, that voice, she pulls herself away, hauls herself up, comes back, panting, numb, she has no idea what just exploded. She tries to convince herself that it is just a story she is telling herself, a horror story, she continues working, and yet . . . that Horror that grabbed her, she knows she didn't invent it, it is too monstrously familiar, it comes from somewhere, from a dungeon covered in polyps, from the lowest depths.

Another afternoon, she goes to the movies with her boyfriend. When the closing credits roll, the vice brutally grabs her throat. She's suffocating, she can't settle her breathing, she pulls herself out of her seat, she hurries, she needs to get out, she bangs into the walls, into the people, "Let me through", she falls to her knees on the pavement outside, her hands pressed against her mouth.

Her boyfriend panics, shouts, "Will you fucking calm down", and smashes his fist into a post. Silence. All it took was a blow for her to become the nice girl again, repentant and guilty and so much easier to live with. For him.

Another time, one among many others, a brutal attack in the middle of a street and no church, no toilets, no enclosed space where she might hide, she can't take another step, she slaps herself with all her strength to come back to herself, to return to the present and catch her breath, she hangs on to a doorway, she's suffocating, she slips, she is in so much pain, she's going to die with her face pressed onto a stone step that stinks of urine. Then just like every other time, it gradually passes, she gets up, tidies her hair, rubs her cheeks and takes up her place again in the file of passers-by.

She hears about a bodywork therapy using touch, and tries it out. Session after session, she lies on a massage table in her pants, under the precise fingers of a generous woman, and learns how to tense or relax more and more precise parts of her body, to feel the atmosphere that settles inside her when she tightens them. She sets herself two goals: to find her pelvis again, and to stop exhausting herself by trying to please all the men she comes across.

At the beginning of the summer, at a psychotherapy session, she is particularly downcast. She concentrates, she goes down into her body, one sensation after another, burning throat, absent heart, knotted stomach, she goes down further, nothing, except yes, the little girl on the ice floe, waiting. As usual.

she squirms curls up one hand pressed
to her mouth the other on her vulva
he is rubbing my vulva
she has no idea who, or where, no context, only the terror of a big man's hand on her little child's vulva and this sentence,

This is going to be good for you.

She feels so small, so defenceless, she discards the hypothesis of the man in the stairwell, the man in the month of May. She remembers him, it wasn't that bad, sure he put his hand in her knickers and put her little hand in his underpants, but she has no memory of feeling so terrified, so sick, she can't remember feeling anything at all, and anyway it was only "sexual contact".

Day after day, night after night, she goes through all the men in her childhood. She doesn't say anything to the guitarist. She keeps her fake smile on. She buries the Horror inside her.

Later on, she joins him on Majorca, where he is rehearsing with his jazz group. She has bought pretty dresses, planning for a salvage and seduction operation that comes to a halt on their first evening under the stars. They haven't even started their romantic dinner when he breaks up with her. They have dinner anyway, walk along the beach, talk, cry.

She burns up the rest of the summer at one party after another, filling herself with alcohol. She would like to eat up all the men she passes to fill the void, to populate the ice floe, but her distress is too obvious to be attractive. She loses six kilos in a month.

When she gets back to Paris, she leaves the cosy cocoon of her parents' home and moves into a flat by herself. Every week, she spends two days at the *École du Jeu*, an hour at psychotherapy, another hour at bodywork. She takes part in three other Family Constellation weekends, takes a course on the issue of self-image, consults an energy specialist, takes Bach flowers, gets her aura cleaned by correspondence. She seeks. She fights.

ON THE EVE OF HER twenty-seventh birthday, she
writes:

I don't know the path that is carrying me forwards,
but I want to feel like myself at last, to look like
that photo taken while I was sleeping, where a
thousand unknown shadows were dancing across
my face. Maybe this pathway, whose contours are
becoming clearer, less blurry, maybe this is just
another mirage. But I have gone too far forwards to
be able to retrace my steps, and even if this road
is uncertain, even if the fog only retreats for a few
centimetres at a time, this is the road I have chosen
and whose first tracks I dug with my tears, my
doubt, my rage and my insatiable curiosity.

During her bodywork therapy sessions, as soon as she
has to tense or relax the inside of her thighs, her lower
abdomen, her perineum: nausea and acid reflux. The
practitioner asks her whether she has been the victim of

any sexual violence, so she confides to her about the "sexual contact" with the man in the stairwell, one Sunday in May, and also that other memory that arose in therapy the previous year, a big man's hand on her little vulva, but whose hand it was and when, she still doesn't know.

A few months later, during a session, while working again and again on the sense of disgust, brutally, her body revulses

between her thighs
a big rough hand bashing her vulva bashing
fingers forcing and going inside
the pain of a fingernail on the vagina walls

he is inside me he put his fingers inside it's him

Terror, hate, violence, contempt, disgust,
pain, power, perversion.
All mixed up. All confused.

She is in the stairwell of her building, everything is intact, like the bedroom of a dead child where the teddy is still lying on the pillow and uncapped felt-tips on the little desk.

She buries herself in bed for ten days, broken to pieces, and invents a massive 'flu so no-one suspects anything. She congratulates herself on no longer living with her parents and on being single.

*

After that session, she feels the fingers inside her a thousand times a day, every day. In her palm, the trace of a moist penis. Discreetly, so no-one can see, she bites her cheeks, her lips, she pinches herself, she digs her nails into the flesh of her finger pads, she rips out her eyebrows, she wipes her hand on her trousers. She needs to get rid of the burn at the entrance to her vagina and the dirty wetness in the hollow of her palm. She continues to hold conversations, to work, to laugh. She manages somehow.

A director tells her, "You are shrinking yourself, you're too juvenile, you're constructing your presence on the basis of your inner child. You need to be more anchored in your sexuality." But what is her sexuality? A few days earlier, she had happily gone round to a friend's place to give him a blow job, spat the sperm out in the sink, brushed her teeth and gone home. To binge. She acts like a libertine and then stuffs as many gnocchi into her mouth as it can hold. She hates fellatio. She hates the smell of men's genitals and when she puts her face too close, she feels as if she is about to throw up. If the man presses her head, she feels like murdering him, then she absents herself and there is nothing left of her but a nice doll. She knows nothing of solitary pleasures except soiled lonesomeness, degrading herself in the secrecy of bathrooms. And yet she would so love to be the flirty redhead, the voluptuous liberated woman who some people see in her. She would like to experience the kind of sexuality that is joyful, simple and shared, but no matter what she does, she is either the frightened virgin, the sex bomb, the frigid woman, the nymphomaniac, the submissive, the whore or the Madonna. She knows all too well that none of these stereotypes she performs is "her". She has no idea what the words "woman" or "women's sexuality" might possibly mean, she is a woman in a civilisation built by men, she knows her own sexuality only in the context of theirs.

She falls in love almost every month. Like Sleeping Beauty, she is waiting for each kiss to wake her, to heal her, and for a few weeks, a few days, all of them are her Prince Charming. She is filled with wonder, she opens up, "Oh darling I never felt anything as strongly as this before you came along", and the jellyfish flee. But she is so happy and passionate in their arms that they feel it's too much, they feel overwhelmed, and then they cut and run. Or else they are fascinated and entranced, and she breaks their heart when the charm evaporates. Then she falls back into the usual hateful slumber, until the next pair of lips.

THAT SPRING, SHE STARTS a novel. A woman has her head shaved at the Liberation, she is in love, he is German.

She is twenty-eight, she tells herself that if she keeps waiting to feel better before she can write, she never will.

Over a few film shoots, she makes friends with a fascinating guy, in his sixties, she takes a while to understand that what he really wants is something to fuck. That old refrain of the guys in the industry, "You are amazing, you have so much talent, I want to help you break through", and then their hands between her thighs. She has heard this so often, too often, she is fed up with their contingent promises, fed up with pushing away their hands, fed up with it being her, every time, who has to apologise.

After a few sessions with a new nutritionist, she is eating better, but while her binges are not quite as frequent, the constant worry about whether and what to eat is a burden, and so she devotes her sixteenth day of Family

Constellations to the issue of bulimia. The next morning, she comes to a stop right in the middle of her bowl of cereal. She is no longer hungry. She cannot remember ever having felt this way, sated, this delicate satisfaction of stopping when she's had enough.

In one meal after another, she discovers the pleasure of food, the incredible refinement of savouring a dish slowly, of salivating ahead of it, of relishing it, of letting the aromas spread inside her mouth without pushing them away with another mouthful. She also discovers that her new-found greediness always comes with an incredible pain in her jaws. She manages somehow.

At the beginning of summer, at a wedding where she knows nobody, and where she was afraid of being really bored, she meets a tall guy she immediately falls in love with. She feels intimidated by the intensity of the emotion and by this sensitive, funny man who appears as intimidated as she is. He warns her, he is ten years older, has two children, and probably needs to go and see a shrink sometime soon. They court in an old-fashioned way, two months before they even dare to kiss. She is a long way from her lightning conquests and Kleenex men.

As the months go by, their love lifts her up and all at once everything seems possible. She is hired for four shows by very different directors whose worlds and words she loves, she travels, she gathers research and ideas for her novel, she has a go at slam poetry. She'd like all the stories mouldering inside her for so long to burst out at last.

And so, yes, there are the inexplicable anxiety attacks, the burn in the hollow of her vagina a thousand times a day, the constant vigilance towards herself and her surroundings, the imperious temptation to flagellate herself, the repeated absences during conversations, the exhausting need to exist in men's gazes, the pains in her jaws. But she gives herself permission, looks to the future, plans for the day after tomorrow, and on stage, she lets the lines and the characters fill her completely. She is often happy. She is proud of all the work she has done to get there.

She has the feeling she is starting to find her way through.

THE HISTORICAL RESEARCH FOR her novel is complete, the first chapters are taking shape, but as one paragraph follows another, she becomes frightened. When she is writing, her head starts spinning, the words slip between her fingers, she can't hold them back and soon there will be none left, no words, she'll be stuck there, mute, waiting on the ice floe. Always judging and constraining herself, she fiddles with each of her sentences so much that she ends up writing no more than a few tiny piles of sand.

One day at rehearsal, someone comes into the theatre through the open doors and steals her computer, and along with it all the research and first scraps of her novel, the story of *Jeanne*, some short stories, poems, scattered pieces. She had never backed anything up, never printed anything off, never sent anything, never read a line to anyone. The jellyfish spread their umbrellas wide and let their silky filaments dance in the icy waters. From now on, as soon as she sits down to write, she feels them crowding into her torso, as soon as she puts down a few words, they press in, they pile up, they rise into her throat, they suffocate her. She is afraid they will spill out of her mouth and invade the horizon for ever. She stops writing.

For a few years now, she has been sharing her love of reading and storytelling with underprivileged children. She loves it, but she is looking for a more political activity, so she joins a feminist company that leads workshops on gender equality. During her training, she attends a conference about sexual violence. She is stunned by what she learns, stunned also to be hearing all this for the first time. She takes eighteen pages of notes:

> The traumatic impact of violence depends on the confrontation of the victim with the destructive intentionality of the assailant, absolutely not on her own personality, or indeed even on the events themselves!
> All assailants use the same predatory strategies to isolate their victims and force them into silence, in order to assure their impunity!

A fascinating psychiatrist, a specialist in caring for victims of sexual violence, masterfully explains how the brain disconnects during a rape, how traumatic memory of the event is created and buried, and the massive consequences this has for the victims' health, sexuality and social lives.

She notes the words "dissociation, high-risk behaviour, avoidance behaviour, panic attacks, self-harm, recurring nightmares, sensations of penetration". She notes, "Victims do not understand any of these symptoms at all. The younger they are when the assault takes place, the more amnesia and post-traumatic stress occur, and the less the connection between the panic attacks and the past assault is recognised."

She avidly takes notes, but she still doesn't recognise the connection.

ON HER THIRTIETH BIRTHDAY, a friend takes
her to a café where you can get free tarot readings, as
long as you get there early and are prepared to wait for
a long time. She needs to think about a question that
means a lot to her. She asks, "What is stopping me from
writing?"

It's her turn, the tarot reader has three students by his
side, who nod every time he says anything, he peers at
her, throws down a few cards, asks a few questions, draws
up a diagnosis: as long as she represents the incarnation
of her grandfather for her mother, she will not find
fulfilment in life. He prescribes her "a psycho-magical
act": she must enlarge a photograph of her maternal
grandfather's face, the family hero, and make a mask out
of it. Dress up as a legionnaire, put on the mask and
the white kepi, and surprise her mother in this disguise
and announce, "I am your father." Then say, "Take off
this mask, take off my clothes", and once she is completely naked, "I am your daughter, you are seeing me
for the first time." Then get dressed, but in women's

clothing, lace, a dress, high heels. Tear up the photo mask with her mother, dig a hole in the earth to bury the shreds, plant a green plant on top. This is the only way she will be able to write and find fulfilment in life, a life which will then be "exciting and brilliant". She feels like bursting out laughing, but everyone is looking at her so seriously. She shivers, she is lost. The tarot reader seizes her hand, "If you want self-fulfilment, if you want to write, do exactly as I say, it's your only way out. Once an act is prescribed, it must be accomplished."

I didn't do it. I did not rock up to my parents' elegant living room disguised a hero of Free France talking like Darth Vader. My grandfather, killed in Indochina a few months before my mother's birth, I had already exhumed him a thousand times in therapy, I had plumbed and plumbed the depths of each impact, just as I had tried to autopsy everything on so many cadavers, just as I had broken into so many closets, drummed my fists on so many doors. I wanted to understand what was wrong with me and why it never got any better, and that tarot-reading charlatan could certainly feel that, and made my entire life depend on a nasty pantomime.

A little later, she moves in with her lover, into an apartment that has enough room for his two children, of whom he has shared custody, and she ventures into the emotional quicksand of the role of stepmother. She can't get over how lucky she is with this wonderfully attentive and gentle man, or the disconcerting simplicity of suddenly sharing love.

That autumn, during a week of training with the feminist company, there is an afternoon session about the criminal law framework for violence against women. It's afternoon tea time, biscuits and teabags litter the table, everyone conscientiously writes in their notebooks that moral harassment, sexual harassment and sexual assault are considered misdemeanours, or minor offences, and are therefore dealt with by the Correctional Tribunal, with its three judges. Whereas rape, murder and torture are considered crimes, and therefore judged in the Assizes Court, by three judges and six jurors selected at random.

The director reads the articles of law to them: "Any act of sexual penetration, of any nature, committed on another person through violence, coercion, threat, or surprise is rape." She defines each term precisely, "Penetration can be characterised as non-consensual fellatio, as vaginal fingering, or as

as vaginal fingering?

Words like lightning bolts piercing the sky.

*

What she has been calling "unwanted sexual contact" for over twenty years, his fingers inside her, his fingers rediscovered inside her four years ago and every single day since, is RAPE. Maybe she isn't so crazy after all, maybe there is a reason for her suffering? Someone hurt her, someone did that word to her. What if the key she has been searching for all these years, all these years of seeking in vain, what if the key was that word?

II

SHE IS THIRTY-ONE YEARS old, making progress, feeling better. But every time she manages to taste a crumb of presence, she is overcome by leaden exhaustion. A few dreary, downcast days always tag along after her discoveries as well as her joys.

One day she talks to her psychotherapist about the violent images where she sees herself dead at every street corner, crushed, dismembered, eviscerated, several times a day, every day. "Nothing serious, but now that I'm biking in Paris, it's annoying, it distracts me." He is dumbfounded. Why did she never tell him about this before, in their nearly ten years of therapy work together? It's her turn to be taken aback. "I'm so used to it, I don't even pay attention to it." She smiles sheepishly. "I thought there was nothing to say. No, I can't remember precisely when it started. When I was a teenager, I already found it hard to concentrate, the images appeared all the time. But really, it's not that bad, it's mostly when I'm on my bike that it bothers me."

There are so many horrors that she doesn't tell

him about, that it would never even occur to her to tell him about.

With the feminist company, she leads writing and drama workshops in high schools in the Paris suburbs. Because she has to spend a lot of time on public transport, she picks up her old tricks from her teenage years: wearing a scarf to discourage men from looking at her breasts, planting her bottom against the doors to avoid peak-time gropers, keeping her head and her eyes down, reading a book or being absorbed in her phone, making herself look unavailable. She has lost count of the flashers, the catcallers and the gropers she has encountered in her city life, the guys in cars who slow down to ask for directions with their penis hanging out, the guys who sit down across from her and masturbate so that she is the only one who can see them, the guys who tell her in detail how they would fuck her and how hard they are, just thinking of her pussy, the guys who insult her mother and grandmother's sexuality because she won't give them her mobile number, the guys who. She knows all about the impunity of men in public spaces.

One evening at the Luxembourg R.E.R. station, a dozen or so toffs in kilts get into her carriage. They are celebrating a rugby match with booze and obscene songs extolling rape and physical violence against women. They are proud of themselves, bellowing lyrics of such brutality that she curls up and puts her hands over her ears. She wishes all the women in the train would stand up with her and force them to be quiet, but she doesn't even dare raise her head. One of them, looking quite the dynamic young executive, ironed shirt, glasses askew, comes up to her and spits out:

> On the ramparts of cunt,
> No, this is not the Devil,
> The ramparts of cunt,
> No, this is not the Devil,
> It's my great hairy junk,
> The ramparts, the ramparts,
> It's my great hairy junk,
> The ramparts of cunt.
>
> On the ramparts of cunt,
> It hardens, and discharges,
> The ramparts of cunt,
> It hardens, and discharges,
> And shoots cum up your cunt,
> The ramparts, the ramparts
> And shoots cum up your cunt,
> The ramparts of cunt.

No-one does anything, she escapes at the next station, runs, sobs, she is so fed up with these men that measure the size of their cocks by the fear they can cause.

*

Throughout the exercises in her workshops, she supports young people learning to sort out words that judge and words that name, those that ring clear and those that feel forced. She follows the blossoming of young women who suddenly blush purple when they discover how subjugated they are. She learns to recognise victims' symptoms, to establish the trust that allows troubles to be told and crimes to be denounced, often for the first time. She discovers how to ensure they are referred for follow-up to competent people, how to report misdemeanours, crimes and damage, and how to point helpless partners towards trustworthy community associations. As the workshops go by, all that pile of words she encountered in her training – sexism, homophobia, domestic violence, child victims and witnesses, corporal punishment, incest, female genital mutilation, forced marriage, polygamy, sexual harassment, sexual assault, rape, gang rape – all of these words become the stories of amazing girls and boys, who make her heart swell with love, such courageous young women and men, with dazzling smiles and appalling stories. And as their trembling words turn into accusing words, she feels the shame deep inside her thinning out and anger rising up, she feels her own head filling with phrases and her cheeks puffing out with words kept silent for far too long.

With her lover, the timidity of the early phases has dissipated, they don't need alcohol anymore to embrace each other. If she isn't drunk, every time his penis is at the opening to her vagina, she bites her lips, she tenses up, she stiffens, she wants to stay there, she doesn't let herself be submerged by disgust, she tries to ignore the fingers. She clings to the look in the eyes of the man she loves, together they will cross this putrid threshold, they kiss again. She told him, she had to, he wondered who the monster is who invites himself into their bed every time. He learns how to cope with their *ménage à trois*.

They marry in early summer. She has the feeling of belonging, at last, of being part of the same world as everyone else. During the wedding speeches, a little of the long veil she had drawn between herself and her family is torn away, that veil she imagined them all standing behind, smiling at her with their hands covering their eyes, and with big eyes drawn on the backs of their hands looking at her without seeing her. She had never been light-hearted at family meals, had often browbeaten them with intractable convictions and sterile arguments. She had felt pigeonholed as the hypersensitive, vulnerable, intolerant one, the one who could have made something of herself but prefers to give workshops to teenagers out in the banlieues, the ungrateful one who is always complaining when she really does have it all. And she judged them too, she also looked at them without seeing them. The veil was opaque in both directions. Her father's eyes glisten when he praises her "irrepressible joie de vivre", and he stresses with a smile her "strange affection for therapists, which might seem a bit odd, but then our ancestors did have their priests and confessors". In her brother's barbs, she hears how her anger and her absences might have been incomprehensible and hurtful, "You don't always realise it when you're the baby of the family, but just ask anyone you know, you received a lot of love, you had the good fortune of living in a loving home."

She gets pregnant very soon afterwards, and in her third month, suddenly the hostile jellyfish reappear and throw themselves at her with no warning. She has terrifying panic attacks she can only stop by slapping herself, banging her head against the walls, splashing herself with cold water.

She increases the frequency of her therapy sessions; she's afraid her madness will kill them both, her and the baby. And during a session spent immersing herself in this fear, she finally manages to express it: "My uterus is my sanctuary, it's like it's the only part of me that hasn't been sullied, that still belongs to me alone, and so if a little penis is floating in there, that's it, there's nothing left of me, I disappear."

She cannot understand why she still feels so dirty, but the sessions make her feel better, her husband is supportive, they regularly see an amazing midwife who practices a touch-based therapy and gives good advice, so the jellyfish float away again.

ONE WINTER'S EVENING, WHEN she is five months pregnant, when she's just popping home for a minute, the landline telephone rings. She never usually answers calls from double-glazing marketers, but this time, she picks it up.

"Good evening, may I speak to Adélaïde Bon please?"

"That's me!"

"Born in Paris on March 1, 1981?"

"Yes. Why?"

"Good evening, Madame. Captain Vidocq speaking."

She bursts out laughing.

"No, Madame, this is not a joke, I'm from the Minors' Protection Unit."

"Oh, I'm sorry, I didn't hear you properly, I thought it was one of my husband's jokes . . ."

"Ah yes, never mind. You reported a sexual assault in 1990, is that right?"

"Um . . . yes."

"Well, I'm calling you to let you know that we have arrested a suspect in this case. I will contact you again in due course so that you can come and make another report."

Maybe he added something else, but that's all she remembers, all she could hold. She's shaking, she presses her forehead, her cheeks, her hands against the window pane, she's burning, she wants to laugh, to cry, to jump, to fall to the floor. All these years, the police hadn't forgotten either? All these years, the police hadn't abandoned her?

She calls her parents, her brother, her two sisters, her husband. She tells them she has just received the best Christmas present in her whole life, she sobs, she is so happy. Her older sister, "It's crazy how sensitive you still are about this, it's ancient history isn't it?"

It has been twenty years or more since they have spoken about it. She had slipped the new word, "rape", into a conversation with her parents in the car, into another one with her sisters in a restaurant. That was when the younger of the two had said her summer lover had raped her when she was a teenager. She hadn't said anything. How do you name such a thing at sixteen, the thing that in one instant and maybe for ever, was enough to destroy everything – love, trust, lightness? What words could she have used? Who would have listened? Who would have believed her? It had taken her years as well, to put the word "rape" to the disaster.

Her sister, her darling sister. They didn't give each other a hug, they didn't dare; a few words in common are not enough to undo so many years of reticence and solitude. When her sister added that a sex therapist she had consulted recently had said "that was not what was wrong with her", she bluntly retorted that that sex therapist was incompetent, and then fell silent.

Two months after the telephone call, she has an appointment with the Minors' Protection Unit to make an updated report. She waits in a café for the distracted friend who is supposed to come help her prepare, but who only arrives in time to go there with her. The captain has asked for a photograph of her at nine years old, so she has two large class photos in her handbag. To calm her fears and impatience, she takes out the two photos and sets them down side by side on the table. In one of them, taken four months afterwards, a cheeky little girl with laughing eyes and a few freckles on her nose. In the second one, sixteen months later, another little girl, her eyes blank, her cheeks drooping, her smile forced. Her dimples have disappeared, she has gained weight, she looks terribly kind.

She stares at the cheeky little girl. She doesn't recognise her. She caresses the photo with her fingertips, follows the oval of the face, doesn't dare touch the eyes, the mouth. She's shaking. That child looking at her, a stranger.

She is sitting in the captain's office, she clings to her pregnant belly, the new life developing inside it, the kindly look of the police officer, the details of the office, the elbow rests, the walls, she's afraid she'll slip. The captain, "You were the victim of a sexual assault in your building, what do you remember?" She can hardly breathe.

"It's a Sunday, the day of the school fête, I'm in *CM1*, or *huitième*, as they call it in my neighbourhood, in the sixteenth arrondissement. It's a beautiful sunny day in May, I'm wearing a white blouse with a round collar and my pretty red pinafore dress with polka dots that my mother made for me, my arms and legs are bare, I have white socks with lace trim and white sandals.

"That morning, after mass, I won a goldfish at the tin can alley. I took it home triumphantly, holding it up high in its plastic bag bursting with water and joy. My brother, my two sisters, my parents were all with me, we did most things together. On weekdays we would always go out with an au-pair girl.

"That afternoon, I begged my parents to let me go back to the fête to buy some food flakes for the gold-fish. 'Just this once,' (you see how little it took for it to happen at that time), 'just this once, Maman, Papa, I'm nine years old, I can go back there by myself, I'm nine, come on.'

"I was allowed to go back there, and with the

remaining change, I secretly bought three Carambar toffees too. I was a little ashamed, I hoped baby Jesus wouldn't come and rap me over the knuckles.

"On the way home, a man follows me and asks the time, I show him my bare arms, I don't have a watch. He has a singsong voice, he tells me to wait a little with him, I tell him, 'My maman says I mustn't talk to strangers', we are already at the front door of my building, he comes in as well, to 'get into the shade for a bit'. He tells me he needs to deliver a bicycle for a girl, about so high, about as tall as I am, who lives in my building in fact. He is kind, he is persuasive. I think that baby Jesus has sent him to give me a chance to redeem my naughtiness with the toffees. He gets into the lift with me and pushes a button. When it stops, he grabs me by the wrist and forces me to get out with him. He hurts me. 'Be a good girl and show me where she lives', I'm frightened, I climb the steps in front of him, not daring to refuse, but as if in slow motion already. Between two floors, he stops. 'You're the same size, aren't you?' Yes. 'Well maybe it would be simpler if I measured the size of the saddle on you rather than disturbing them on a Sunday?' Yes. 'You have to lift up your dress so I can measure.' Yes. Or maybe then I didn't say anything anymore."

She tries to tell what happens next, but the fragments that remain are not coherent, she doesn't know anymore whether it was him or her who lifted up the dress, she says, "He puts his hand in my knickers", but she remembers she wasn't wearing knickers by then. When did he pull them down?

She says, "I remember that he had a crocodile skin belt with a gold buckle, which he loosened when he took his penis out of his trousers," but she doesn't remember his penis.

She says, "He made me take his penis in my hand, he made me move my hand over it."
The captain, "Stroking it?" No, not at all, that's not what stroking is. But she has to agree to sully the word since there is no other, since there is no word that can express all the ugliness of the back-and-forth movement of a little child's hand on an adult's stiff penis.

She says, "He put his fingers inside me, I remember his finger moving around inside me." She doesn't dare use the word "rape", she expects him, the policeman, to say it. He takes detailed notes, doesn't say anything.

She says, "I was on the step above him, he was facing me."

She says, "There was some noise downstairs, someone came into the building or else the concierge went out of her flat. He stopped." I know now that there was no noise downstairs. He didn't stop. She invented the noise story, long ago, to protect herself from what he did to her, afterwards.

She says, "He took my hand and wiped it on his trousers."

The captain compares her account with the one she gave on the day of the events. She had said, "He was behind me", she has just said the opposite. "I don't know. He must have changed positions." When? She had said, "He touched my bottom: front and back." Back? She doesn't remember. "He said I have a big bottom. He put his willy between my legs. I was really frightened." His penis between her legs? She can't remember anymore.

The captain asks her to describe him, she can clearly see his pale blue shirt with short sleeves, his clinking croco-dile skin belt, his vaguely vintage grey canvas trousers, but she does not remember his penis, his hands, his eyes, she doesn't remember how he looked at her, or the expression on his face. The image is blurred in places like in the crime scenes on television.

The captain shows her a set of photographs where four bald men are looking at her. Police custody images, taken standing face-on, bags under the eyes, hard lips. She hesitates. She is not sure. Twenty-three years have gone by, the face she remembers seems to have holes instead of eyes, and at nine years old, she was barely 1.3 metres tall, she saw him from below, like in a low-angle camera shot.

The captain points to one of the four sinister faces: the man in the stairwell, the man in the merry month of May, the one the police nicknamed "the electrician", a long face, the captain says that's him, his name is Giovanni Costa. She is hesitant. She is hopeful.

Over the following days, she finds a few online articles from the press after his arrest. "The man operated in rich neighbourhoods in the capital, often presenting himself as an electrician needing a hand to reach a fuse box or a light bulb."

She looks at the comments, or rather, at the exchanges of anonymous invective. One man is happy, "Serves those dirty bourgeois right, you can bet they really turned him on, those bourgeois little bitches." She sighs. She thinks about that stinging email she received a few months earlier from an envious friend, "What a hard road poor beautiful Adélaïde has had, born with a silver spoon in her mouth (or was it gold?), and who still starts complaining and making a fuss! Your childhood was not that bad, everything was easy for you, so that's enough now, O.K., you know there are lots of people who have had much harder lives that yours."

Granted. While money didn't buy me happiness, it did allow me to pay for a psychotherapist all these years, it did give me the time I needed to try to get better, and it's just as well I was a "bourgeois little bitch".

SHE IS THIRTY-TWO, AND preparing to give birth as well as can be expected, with the body-therapy midwife and another militant feminist midwife, who is the wonderful facilitator of an antenatal group. She is just starting her last month of pregnancy when the panic attacks come crashing back. The closer she gets to her due date, the more frightened she becomes. She's afraid that the fingers will slide inside her during delivery and hurt the baby.

One day, sobbing after a new attack that has left her drained and exhausted, she calls the feminist midwife and is given an appointment for the next day with no further questions. And so, clutching her husband's hand, she tells the story of the man in the month of May, the panic attacks, the fingers, the visceral terror that the child will be soiled if he passes down there. She's afraid of the epidural, of not feeling her pelvis when she has spent so many years trying to find it again, afraid of being absent at the crucial moment when her baby will need

127

her so much, afraid that the fingers will suffocate the baby. Her husband talks about his own desperation, his powerlessness. The midwife listens to them, reassures them, explains how this kind of anxiety is common in women who have been victims of sexual violence. She advises her to deliver without an epidural, to keep contact with the baby, with herself, she gives them precious advice about dealing with the pain. The bodywork midwife gives them the same advice, and trains her husband to support her with his hands and his eyes, and her to breathe, to sing each contraction, to feel the baby inside her, to help it to descend in the right direction.

When the first labour pains start, on a beautiful sunny day in the month of May, she feels confident, ready, present. Her voice accompanies each contraction with a deep, powerful chant, and the obstetric nurses slip their heads through the doorway to encourage this Zen master.

No trace of the man in the stairwell that day, that wonderful day, that day in the merry month of May, that day my son was born.

SHE IS A YOUNG mother, a wide stretch of downy skin to nurse her tiny child, enormous ears listening to his every breath, she-wolf's teeth to protect him from witches, lynx's eyes, huge heavy breasts. In this tender milky paradise, monstrous jellyfish are lying in wait. This is the beginning of the blank months.

At the beginning of autumn, death enters without knocking at her psychotherapist's door, the one who has been supporting her for eleven years. They had stopped seeing each other for a few months, just while she was caring for her new-born baby, they were going to start up again soon.

In a little country cemetery with fields all around, she buries a friend, a mentor, a father. She must take off her harness and climb down the cliff-face alone, through the fissures, to the depths of the crevices. He was the only person in the world with whom she felt safe, the only one to whom she had dared to describe a few of the jellyfish, the only one to have ventured onto the ice floe beside her.

His room at the back of the courtyard, that comforting island where she could catch her breath, is gone. She drifts, as the jellyfish buffet her along in the currents.

She signs up for a creative writing workshop, on the mezzanine of a feminist bookshop in rue de Charonne. She's looking for a safe harbour where she can unload some of the bric-a-brac of sentences piling up inside her head in vain. She is too afraid to write when she is alone.

After a few months, she is ashamed to realise that, no matter what prompt or constraint she is given, whether directly or implicitly, she only ever writes about the afternoon in May when she was nine years old, and about him, the man in the stairwell.

One Saturday, the directions are to start with an anonymous opening line, chosen from a selection. She doesn't hesitate, she knows straight away which one she will choose, without ever having read it before, without knowing which work it opens, she grasps it as one grasps an outstretched hand when falling, and she writes these words in one burst, without stopping, crossing out, or editing:

"The morning I got up to begin this book I coughed."

Like a gangue which starts to crack at last under the violence of a first spasm.

As far back as my memories carry me, I have put my hands to my throat when I feel strong emotion. I palp it, I hold it, and calm returns to me, the storm dissipates. My doorway-throat, the decompression chamber between inside and outside, which allows me to put together this appealing smiling face, these laughing eyes, these charming dimples, this "agreeable person" under all circumstances.

On the hooks on my vocal cords, I hang all my rage, hatred, disgust, contempt for myself and others, and then my softened voice is disguised by harmonious modulations. Don't let anything show, don't let anything be heard. Let the turmoil bash my diaphragm and my ribs, let the blizzard rage in my pelvis, don't stop the claws digging into my aorta, cut myself loose from this numb and bloody torso.

My throat, a fireman's ladder to escape from disaster, to get away, to float.

And yet, every morning when I wake up, that nasty taste of blood, that need to yawn so wide, so wild, to open up my throat with forceps and allow me to vomit you at last.

For it's you, it's you who reigns in my breast and who controls my throat. Because ever since that day, and those minutes outside myself, I am yours. Or you are in me, for I don't know the difference anymore. I am your meal always being served, and there is nothing left of me except a container, the flask from which your ghost drinks deep every day. And under my fixed and smiling face, the rage in my blood is all that is left to me of life. Of any life at all. Of a life of my own.

And writing this makes my heart beat so fast that I'm afraid that if I cough, my throat will let that rage escape and spill out over the paper.

And I imagine it, foul, ghastly, festering with pus and malignant humours, and I'm afraid it will leap out and go wandering, assault a passer-by and force a way down their throat and the coughing starts up again and I start barking in the icy silence of this apartment. My hand is clutching the words it is tracing, for writing about you is the only thing that gives me back a voice, any voice at all, a voice of my own. Once the book goes to press, I won't bark anymore. I'll have other things to say at last.

It's her turn to read, she hesitates, and in that hesitation, in the tiny lapse of time that precedes her decision to read aloud, she understands that it is time for her to write to be read. This will be the foundation text, the opening lines of many words to come, the first I will share with a few friends, that I will read to a small gathering of strangers on the last day of the workshop, that I will send to a competition, without success as it turns out.

It was the hand of Anaïs Nin I grasped that day, and with those first words of her novel *House of Incest*, she certainly helped me up, through the mysterious sisterhood suddenly woven between her words and mine.

SINCE THE POLICEMAN'S TELEPHONE call, or perhaps it is since the birth of the miracle child, the jellyfish have mutated and the images are more terrifying than ever. Her days are busy and full of joy, then without warning, they explode.

How to contain the horror in words. How to tell about the blank months. My son, my love, my darling, he might read these words one day. He will be hurt and I don't know if I will be able to fix him, to console him from that kind of hurt. But I will write these words anyway, I owe them to myself, I owe them to the little girl waiting for me on the ice floe, I owe them to all the lives of pain.

at the movies a rape scene with torture
her neighbours repelled her vulva swollen
in the bath skin to skin with her baby,
imagining masturbating him
wanting to tear her head from her body
or drink the bottle of bleach

not being able to breathe anymore
the little one sick at night in the big bed
and his tiny bare feet just next
to her labia
trying to drown herself in the bath
changing the baby's nappy his penis is hard
imagining licking it
wanting to sew up her eyelids
clutching the changing table
so as not to run, climb over the balcony railing, jump
changing the little baby's nappy
avoiding looking at his penis for fear that she might
changing the nappy and singing, telling a story,
making jokes, mostly, more than anything, filling the gaps
a thousand times a day, clenching her teeth,
digging her nails deep into her skin
so that the huge fingers come out of her vagina
buying a vibrator in secret to administer
preventative brutalities to herself before going to her child
avoiding staying alone at home avoiding staying alone
with her little boy avoiding thinking
avoiding thinking avoiding looking at
his little penis avoiding breathing too much avoiding

being lost

The days without crashes are rare. When she is alone
at home, first she feels the big fingers inside her, then

something else that is about to happen and that terrifies her. She's suffocating, she can't breathe, so, like an automaton, she quickly sets up what she needs for it to stop: get the vibrator, close the curtains, pull down her trousers, her pants, enter "porn video rape" into Google (erotic short stories haven't been enough for a long time, they're not violent enough) then she insults herself, degrades herself, brutalises herself. In the throbbing of the blood vessels in her inflamed vulva, nothing is good, nothing is gentle, nothing is restorative. She watches the screen, and becomes the violence of the man who throws a woman to the ground and holds the back of her neck so she sucks him off, she becomes the woman who controls her gag reflex to show she likes it and could spend hours being penetrated, exposed, degraded that way. After a while, depending on the violence of the images and the intensity of the anxiety that came before, she stops, sated, ashamed, with a painful vulva and a grieving heart. She is absent at last. She spends the following hour drifting between two tides, groggy, nauseated, worried.

Sometimes doing it once is not sufficient to dissolve her for long enough, so she starts again.

She has more and more trouble making love with her husband. He does everything he can to reassure her, with gentleness, with soft words, but as soon as it's about sex, every second is afraid of the next one, when the other man's fingers will find their way between her thighs, and then disgust, and terror. She bites her tongue, digs her nails into the flesh of her fingers, hangs on to the loving gaze, but when the other man is there, she drowns.

One night, they are kissing, blissing out. It explodes. She pushes him away with such violence that she's out of the bed, ashen, haggard. The other man is there, she feels his hands all over her and the revolting smell of his penis, she tries frantically with her little hands to get him off her skin, her mouth, her buttocks, her vulva, she feels sick to her stomach, her eyes are wide, her tongue is trying to vomit itself.

That night comes to haunt all the other nights.

She shares a part of it, the only part that can be put in words, the common, admissible generalities about women victims' anxieties, with a girlfriend, who contacts Dr Salmona, the renowned psychiatrist whose presentation at the conference a few years ago she had found so fascinating.

The psychiatrist can only give her an appointment in the summer, when the holidays will have diluted the gridlock in the waiting room. In the meantime, she reads her book, *The Black Book of Sexual Violence*:

In the absence of treatment and understanding of the mechanisms at the origin of traumatic memory, the victim is subjected to these memories and generally believes them to be psychological productions coming from her own thinking processes, which is particularly frightening.

She will believe that she is terrorised, in a state of panic, about to die, when there is nothing threatening her.

She will believe that she is suddenly depressed, that she has lost hope, and will see committing suicide and disappearing as the only way out, when everything is going well for her, and she loves life.

She will believe that she is guilty and ashamed of what she is, she will think she has no value, that she is ugly, stupid, worthless, a piece of rubbish to be thrown away, when she does everything very well. She will believe she is monstrous, aggressive, perverse, capable of doing evil, when all she wants is to love. She will believe she wants violent and degrading sexual acts, when all she dreams of is tenderness.

Her eyes are burning, her throat is bleeding, she feels like shouting her joy to the moon. Her heart bursts into a thousand golden pieces. All of this long paragraph is her.

The traumatic memory of the violent acts and of the assailant will colonise the victim and be the source of a confusion between herself and the assailant, a confusion which is responsible for feelings of shame and guilt, which will be fed by violent and malignant words, images and emotions, which she wrongly perceives as her own, when they originate with the assailant.

Traumatic memory haunts the victims, dispossesses them and stops them from being themselves, worse still, it makes them believe that they are double, or even triple: a normal person (which they are), a nobody who is afraid of everything, a guilty person they are ashamed of and who deserves to die, a person who could become violent and perverse and who needs to be constantly controlled and censored.

In the time it took to rape me, the man in the stairwell insinuated himself into the folds of my brain, leaving his hate and perversity to macerate in the antechamber of my memory, and day after day, that hate and perversity dribbled down inside me, colonised each of my thoughts, and contaminated my life. An invisible invasion that no-one helped me see, or name, or understand.

Since that Sunday in the month of May, twenty-four years of breaking and entering, anytime, anywhere. Filthy thought after filthy thought, I found myself buried alive, trembling, crushed under my self-loathing and the terror that it could be seen, that it could be known.

And especially this poison-thought, ever since the birth
of my darling child

I could destroy my own son

No. These filthy thoughts do not belong to me. The filth
is all his.

SHE HAS JUST TURNED thirty-three, she makes an appointment with a barrister she has been referred to by the European Association Against Violence Against Women in the Workplace. She wants to have her complaint reclassified, from "unwanted sexual contact" to "rape". That word is necessary for her. She also wants to join the proceedings as a civil claimant seeking damages in her own name, so she can be informed of the progress of the case, and be able to attend the entire trial.

To get to the barrister's chambers, she has to take two flights of steps covered in the same carpet as in her parents' stairway, the blue, red and green carpet of hell, that long carpet found in so many Haussmann-style buildings and that she systematically avoids when she is alone, always taking the lift instead. That day, she takes the stairs and vigorously stamps on the cursed carpet all the way up.

The barrister has a soft voice, a slim and determined figure, a dimple by her nose, piercing eyes. With each question and answer, with one issue after another, she opens up a pathway through the rigours of the law. She explains, "This case covers sexual assaults and rapes, the proceedings will therefore be conducted in the Assizes Court, where three judges and six randomly selected jurors will deliberate on each of the offences." She warns her, "The proceedings can take a long, long time, you will need to arm yourself with patience." And now, roped up together, they draw up a list of witness statements to gather, and documents to produce.

She receives a first Witness Notification. She reads the names of thirty-four other girls and is astounded to know two of them. One was in middle school with her, the other is the big sister of her best friend when she was nine, her best friend, to whom she had said nothing. There are no words, when you're nine, to talk about something like this.

She liked her a lot, that big sister. They had both taken the Drama option one year, when she was in *seconde*, and the sister in *terminale*, and they were both at the heart of a very tight group. She finds her number again, calls her. And as the sluice gates open, the water rushes in, and they tell each other their stories. He said the same words to both of them, that man whose name might be Giovanni Costa. She hangs up, curls up on the big bed, and sobs.

There is another little girl on the ice floe. I will never be alone again.

AT LAST THE SUMMER arrives and with it her first session with the psychiatrist. Her practice is nestled at the back of a courtyard with trees and chirruping birds, and in the waiting room, the words "me too" float with tenderness in some of the eyes. The psychiatrist arrives, she is sorry to be running late, she leads her towards a cluttered desk, sits down, settles, looks at her.

To her, she will tell everything. Everything that she never dared tell anyone, everything that she is so ashamed of, everything that is so loathsome inside her, so crazy, so perverse. The psychiatrist diagnoses "Post-Traumatic Stress Disorder".

As the sessions go by, with the explanations of brain function and traumatic memory, the jellyfish turn into symptoms, into consequences, and the man in the month of May, into a sexual paedo-criminal. She is relieved not to have to use the enemy's word any longer, the lying word: "paedophile".

The first time she reports the facts, she starts with the sunny Sunday, the school fête, the goldfish, the

Carambar toffees and the man who speaks nicely, who takes the lift, who pulls her towards the stairs. Halfway up, she stops, confused. There is nothing left of the rest of it except a few mismatched fragments, always the same ones, that she sees from a distance. Then she is at the top of the stairs. Dressed. When? The threads are broken. There's a snag in her story.

A month later, in the haven of the consulting room, she's trying to remember, she topples over

> *I am in the stairwell he is there he is looking at me*
> *he says words to me that I don't hear*
> *he does things to me that I don't feel*
> *he looks at me*
> *his eyes are icy and metallic*
> *I do not exist in them*
> *I do not exist anymore*
> *I have just ceased to exist*

That look is beyond words. I don't know anything like it, anything in the world, anything that might contain it, express it, describe it. There is no vocabulary for that look.

That look, which was fixed on me.

AFTER ANOTHER MEETING WITH the barrister, she needs to make a list of all the steps she has taken to try to recover. She has kept the little diaries with black leather covers and bible paper from the last fourteen years, so she patiently sets about putting together a record of all her appointments. The results are astounding: 226 individual therapy sessions, 39 group therapy sessions, 21 Family Constellation days, 146 vocal yoga sessions, 118 bodywork therapy sessions, 58 Feldenkrais classes, 16 nutritionist appointments, 37 osteopathy sessions and other varied practices. She doesn't count the drama training or the yoga and Pilates classes, those thousands of hours trying to feel her own body, or the singing or trumpet lessons trying to find her breath, or the essays, the memoirs, the personal development books, the internet sites, all that time spent searching for a light in her infinite sadness.

I have spent a fortune of hours and money to get to where I am today. If I hadn't had places where I could take off my mask year after year, where I could allow myself to cry, to seek, to maintain the hope of getting out of the abyss, if I hadn't been "born with a silver spoon in my mouth", I would probably be long since dead. Or I would have buried myself in a pretend life, a glossy magazine life.

She gathers up her courage in both hands to ask various people to write witness statements about everything she has been through, so that a "body of corroborating evidence" can support the reclassification of her complaint. At first, she gets muddled in timid explanations, she blushes, but the more she talks about it, the more confidence and clarity she gains. A victory.

She meets the midwife who was so supportive at the end of her troubled pregnancy. She agrees with no hesitation, and so will a woman theatre director, her osteopath, and, with heart-rending sincerity, her husband.

She goes back to see the nutritionist who treated her in her late teenage years. On the patient's card found in the archives, the doctor reads that she had diagnosed her with "bulimic hyperphagia". I wish she had said those words to me back then, "bulimic hyperphagia". They would have comforted me. They would have been my first words, they would have been useful later on, and maybe I wouldn't have had to stuff myself for ten more years. I was so hungry for words to make me feel better.

She finds her first bodywork therapist, who becomes emotional as she remembers their work and that session, the violence of her memories, that lively body on the treatment table, those horrifying, astonished words, "he is inside me he put his fingers in my vagina".

Late one morning she goes round to her parents' place, still the same apartment. She is embarrassed to ask her mother for a written statement, but the barrister insisted, "Maybe she remembers the visit to the paediatrician the next morning." She agrees to ask her just to put her mind at rest, without expecting much.

Her little girl's room has become her mother's office, and when they sit down at the secretaire, she sees herself again that day, stunned, curled up on her flowery duvet, pretending to read *Nobody's Child*.

Her mother starts to talk. Yes, she remembers that appointment, she remembers the moment the paediatrician opened her thighs to look at her little vulva, that hovering moment when instead of the line she knew so well for having washed it, put nappies on it, cared for it, instead of that line, there was a space in parentheses. She remembers the paediatrician's words, "That is completely abnormal." Her mother opens a drawer of the secretaire in silence, takes out a blank piece of paper, draws large brackets, grabs a ruler, measures the space between the two signs, "There, it was like that. There was a space of about one to one and a half centimetres."

She whispers, "It's an image that stayed with me, that remained very strong for me. There was something that wasn't right, that didn't make sense, not at all, but there was nothing else, no injuries, no bruises." A beat. "You know, for me, rape was with a man's penis, with punches, with screams. I just didn't even think of it. When you finally told me it was his fingers, that finally made sense of that image." That absurd image, buried in the folds of her memory, that image was waiting for me to come and find it so it could unfold at last and offer me the tangible proof that I am not making anything up, that I am not insane. All those years drumming on doors, and all it took was two parentheses on a piece of paper.

Afterwards we had lunch, just the two of us, at the little table in the dining room facing the Seine, and for the first time, I admitted to her how I had hidden and isolated myself, how afraid I was of being discovered, of being rejected. How I tried to recover, how I fought, how alone I had been. How much I missed them. "And yet, you seemed so happy, you are always smiling and cheerful, everybody says that you are *joie de vivre* incarnate." Yes, I love joy madly, I need joy like I need air, I throw myself in its arms each time it passes. Maybe you need to be very unhappy to be profoundly joyful, maybe joy is the other side of tears. She was listening to me, this sensitive loving woman, and that woman, I suddenly remembered, is Maman, my long-lost Maman, found again at last.

*

Later on, she goes back to the paediatrician who treated her, and her brother and sisters too. He is still practicing, he still has his funny bowl haircut. He is attentive and apologetic. He remembers too, and even if he doesn't say so, he seems to be aware of the blind drifting that the absence of his words, the error in his diagnosis, caused for her that day, and every day since. He writes, "She presented no signs of physical violence (no contusions or ecchymosis). However, the small lips of the vulva showed a vertical opening of 1 to 1.5 cm high with no bleeding, which is totally abnormal for a child of her age, which might have indicated the rupturing of the hymen. Retrospectively, this could indicate vaginal penetration by fingers, which could therefore be considered to be rape."

Considered to be rape. He and my mother are standing amidst the devastation wrought by the myth of "true" rape, the one with screams, blows and injuries, the one where a penis penetrates a vagina, the one perpetrated on lightly-clad young women by libidinous individuals hiding in parking lots. I remember a friend who was horrified to learn that I was raped as a child, and so relieved when I told him it was with fingers. "Oh, O.K., that's not really rape then, it's not as serious really."

And yet, the most frequent rapes are those perpetrated on children, with no other physical violence than penetration. However, no matter where that penetration is, whether it's vaginal, anal or oral, and no matter what means are used, penis, fingers or objects, nearly all persons who have been victims of rape in childhood develop chronic developmental trauma disorders. Having been a victim of sexual violence in childhood is the most significant determining factor in the person's health fifty years later, and can mean a reduction of their life expectancy by up to twenty years. How is it, in our over-informed society, that this information is not freely circulating?

Since her psychotherapist is dead, his partner provides a witness statement regarding the eleven years of individual therapy and the three years of group therapy.

How I would have loved to share with him the shining joy of at last knowing the family name of those jellyfish, polyps and medusas: P.T.S.D. How I would have loved to tell him that those long years spent searching together were not in vain, but allowed me to hang on until now, to have the incredible chance of making a new start in life, of catching it on the wing.

The psychotherapist who was the co-leader of the therapy and Family Constellations groups, a precise and attentive woman, also a sex therapist, a woman whom she deeply trusts, this woman hesitates to make a statement. She invokes sacrosanct professional confidentiality, it's difficult to convince her, to protest that all she is being asked to do is to report the facts. She ends up agreeing, but she says nothing about Family Constellations and reduces the eleven years of individual therapy to "several years". I did not understand why, I still don't. She advises me to "think about the assailant and the rape and ask that energy to go to the furthest reaches of the universe", but I have already done that and it wasn't enough.

She reads her psychiatrist's affidavit a thousand times. "The disorders my patient presents are all compatible with the facts of the sexual violence she describes, and they all enter into the framework of chronic Post-Traumatic Stress Disorder specifically presented by victims of childhood sexual violence. These disorders represent a major handicap and health risk, and require regular psychotherapeutic treatment."

She is diagnosed, she is suffering from something analogous to an illness that can be treated and cured. The jellyfish are pathognomonic symptoms, the jellyfish are the medical proof of what he did to her.

I am not insane, I am not vile, I am not weak, I am not violent. It's just that, one day in the month of May, a man grabbed me and gobbled me up.

ONE MORNING, IN THE psychiatrist's waiting room, a wraithlike woman is sitting across from her. That wraith, she recognises, was her the previous evening. She couldn't sleep, she slid into the water of a forgotten bath, still full of toys, she stayed there rolled up into a ball, gently rocking, her heart like ice. She wishes she could put her arms around this young woman and warm her up, stroke her long dark hair, help her come back to herself. Looking at her pale complexion, her hard features, her empty eyes, she measures her own improvement, how much better she is feeling now. Despite the roller-coaster and the frequent crashes, the absences and self-flagellations, a murmuration of hopes is taking flight.

The psychiatrist advises her to go back to the place where he raped her, in her childhood stairwell. And so, one autumn day, she doesn't drop in to see her parents, she doesn't go and say hello, no, that day she comes to climb the stairs. A girlfriend comes with her, and, so that they don't bump into anyone they know, they go down through the Trocadéro gardens and take the path from the little playground to her house that she took when she was small. She doesn't say much, her heart is heavy. Once inside the building, "I can't remember what floor it was on, let's go upstairs, I'll see." She climbs the stairs and all at once, between two floors, she stops. "It's here." The little white paper bag with the Carambars and the yellow plastic container were set down on the corner of this step, "He stopped here, I was a few steps higher up, just here, and then

> *his eyes*
> *his hard eyes*
> *his big man's hands my dress goes up*
> *my pants go down*
> *his hand takes mine and rubs it*
> *squishy, flaccid, moist, foreign*
> *his other hand between my thighs*
> *his voice says horrid words*
> *like you love this it's nice you're a good girl*
> *you like it don't you I can tell you love it*
> *and*
> *and*

Everything is such a blur after his hard eyes.

"When he was done I went upstairs." And so she goes up a few steps, struggling, as stunned now as she was back then, she concentrates, left, the knee bends and the lower leg goes up and then goes down, right, the foot presses down onto the step, left, right. An automaton following someone's feet – hers? He's following her. A body, suddenly imposed, suddenly the enemy. A completely different body. And time stretches out as she moves upwards, space distends itself, and she feels, she knows, that a few steps down, he destroyed her and her lovely life.

On the landing, she stands still. "He is there, halfway between the floors, doing the let's be friends thing, making me swear, making me promise." She takes a deep breath and goes back down again, goes back to it. With sensitivity, with caution. When she reaches the cursed step, she sits down and holds herself in her own arms. Tenderly. For a long time.

Inside her vagina, the burning has stopped. The big dirty fingers have vanished.

A few days later, after considering the evidence provided, notably the paediatrician's affidavit, the Juge d'Instruction, the investigating judge in charge of preparing the trial, approves the request for reclassification and orders "a supplementary court investigation into the allegation of rape committed against Adélaïde Bon".

Rape. Four letters, and inside them, my return ticket to my native land. Nine-year-olds know nothing about words, nine-year-olds just take words as they come. In the stairwell that day, words were tipped over, I could only speak upside down, and my mother tongue became a foreign language. All these years I've been prattling on, I've been running as fast as I can behind words that forked my tongue, I've been exhausting myself searching for stable words, for yesterday words, for childhood words.

Words draw the horizon of our thoughts, so when words lie, when enemy is replaced by friend, violence by pleasure, rape by contact, paedo-criminal by paedophile, and victim by guilty, the horizon is a line of barbed wire blocking off all the exits to the camp.

SINCE SHE IS JOINING the proceedings as a civil claimant, she prepares herself for a psychological assessment with a court-appointed expert. Her barrister advises her to be concrete, to give details of the symptoms and their consequences for her life, to remember that this assessment will be read to everyone in court. Her psychiatrist recommends that she stay on her guard. Remember that some things victims admit to are all too often turned against them, and that it is very rare for court experts to be trained in the specifics of sexual violence and its consequences. Give nothing away about her private life that is not connected to the rape. Remain evasive about any symptoms that might be severely judged. Try, just this once, not to minimise anything.

When she makes the appointment over the phone, she asks the expert whether she needs to bring any particular documents, such as the medical certificates that led to the reclassification of her complaint. The expert says no, of course she has the whole case file in hand.

*

The office is furnished with such opulence that it's intimidating, but the expert smiles at her. She reads out the various questions she has to answer. She asks about her family, everyone's professions, her childhood, her adolescence. She asks her whether she has ever taken drugs. Suspiciously, "Yes, I tried cannabis, but it amplified my dark thoughts, so I quickly stopped." She does not mention the fact that "quickly" can actually be counted in years, or anything about the other illegal substances she also ingested.

"Dark thoughts? What do you mean by that?"

She explains this with the first memory that comes to her, in *sixième*, when she made an interminable presentation all by herself on the Holocaust.

"Did any of your family members die in concentration camps?"

"No."

"What impact did the war have on your family?"

"One of my grandfathers was a hero of the Liberation, but this fascination with death camps is something else, it's . . ."

The expert is not listening to her, she declares, "It was connected to him, that presentation."

She asks about her education, her professional life.

"Actress, voice artist, facilitator of theatre and creative writing workshops on equal rights for women."

"Oh! I see! Gender theory! But really now . . . Believing

that men and women are identical is just plain stupid, you can see it from childhood onwards, little boys are unruly, little girls play with dolls."

And Adélaïde retorts, already exhausted by all this, "Gender theory does not exist, only gender studies, very diverse, often fascinating studies, where researchers analyse the social constructions of the sexes, not their nature." Over the course of all those workshops, she has seen too much of the human cost of sexist stereotypes, she has plenty of experience to share on the topic, but since the expert is continuing to listen to her own voice lining up one platitude after another, she breathes, she settles down again. She must not reveal anything of her feminist activism, experts often use it to cast doubt on victims' evidence. She waits.

Later on: "You are beautiful, and still young. Your only problem is that you don't love yourself. Love yourself a little more!"

"Loving yourself when you feel soiled is not that easy."

"But you're letting him win by thinking that! You're the one letting him win! You need to fight, to learn how to make the most out of life! Listen, try to enjoy a few little moments of pleasure every day, the Coué self-hypnosis method, it works, you know! You are too sensitive, too fragile. And after all, what is a rape? Fifteen minutes of your life? Fingers in your vagina? You know, there are people all around you who are suffering, who have gone through really terrible things. It's just like accidents and comas, some people come through very well and some people's lives are turned upside down, it depends on their makeup. Look at Marie Laforêt, she was raped too, you know!"

She bursts into tears. The expert keeps going, softly, in the patronising tone often used with little children. "I know I'm provoking you a little, but it's only to help you. You can't give up on yourself. You tell me you're an actress, and it was a last resort, but it's a great thing to be an actress. You are too cerebral, so theatre is a sublimation, it's an excellent choice for you." She concentrates, she settles down, she calms herself. She must not let her guard down. The expert later reiterates the comparison she seems to find particularly pertinent between rape and accidents, and the misguided yet widespread idea that there are people who recover better from sexual violence because they have made a decision to do so.

She relates the facts. At the moment they enter the building: "Didn't anyone ever tell you not to let strangers inside?"

"Um, yes. Of course they did. But he was very nice and I was only nine years old, I had no idea that such nasty people existed."

The expert nods with a knowing expression. "Your childhood was far too sheltered."

When she gets to the murderous glint in the man's eyes, that precise moment when she became dissociated from herself, a brutal terror pierces her with a thousand nails, her mouth opens, no sound comes out, and seeing her like this, paralysed and ghastly white, the expert panics. "Oh no, no, this is not the time, no, this is not the place, you need to pull yourself together now, do you hear me, you need to move on now, and tell me the rest of your story." She makes an incredible effort to come back, to suck in a little air, to unlock her jaws, she manages to get up, to catch her breath, to take a few steps, she apologises, she sits down again. The expert cites La Rochefoucauld, "Neither the sun nor death can be looked at face to face", and analyses, "You saw your death, that's why you have this anxiety, that's what is so difficult for you, not the rape. You absolutely need to work on your fear of death with your psychiatrist. He was not a killer, he wouldn't have killed you, that's just what you believed."

The expert asks her to list her strengths and weaknesses, then she gives her two questionnaires with convoluted and intrusive questions. Something is expected of her but she can't work out what, she has to play a game whose rules she doesn't know, a game where she is the mouse.

To finish, she has to say what she sees in big inkblots. When she gets to the last one, she describes a dead pelvis that can still give life. "Oh well, I'm relieved, everything you said earlier was so horrible! I'm glad we're ending on something a little more positive."

And while she is standing up, putting on her jacket: "O.K., so for the preliminary hearing, you don't have a problem with it, do you?" She freezes.

"A hearing with Giovanni Costa?" The expert nods. "Um yes, I do, of course I have a problem with it, I don't want to meet him face to face."

"But listen, you won't be alone, there will be lawyers there, it's just like at the trial, it will make no difference to you."

"No. No, really, no. It's not the same, it will be in a small group. We'll be face to face. No, I don't want him to look me in the eyes. I'm afraid. I don't feel confident about this."

The expert sighs.

In the corridor, as she takes her to the exit, "The case will probably go to the Correctional Tribunal, it would be much better for you for it to be judged there, by professional judges, rather than a jury. The proceedings will be faster and less painful."

With false naivety – she knows that rapes are downgraded from crimes to misdemeanours to free up the schedules of the Assizes Court – "I thought rapes were only tried at the Assizes Court?"

"Yes, that's right, it would no longer be a rape, but it will still be much better for you."

"But it's important for me that what happened to me is given its name. Didn't you read in the file that I managed to get my complaint reclassified from sexual assault to rape? That the suspect is alleged to have assaulted and raped dozens of little girls? Don't you know they have his D.N.A. for four of them?"

The expert raises her eyebrows and hisses, "The Assizes proceedings will be very hard on you. I hope you're up to it." She sees her out with an icy handshake.

Afterwards, she has two weeks of insomnia, nightmares, bulimia, thoughts of self-harm, two weeks feeling like less than nothing again, two blank weeks.

Her barrister is flabbergasted when she tells her about it later, as she had just received her copy of the expert's report and, for once, it had seemed appropriate. The expert concluded that "her reactions are typical of victims of sexual assault: fear for her life, peri-traumatic dissociation and sexual dysfunction", that "she still presents strong anxiety and a severe state of stress, including anxiety about death". What would have happened if, as usual, she had minimised it all, downplayed it, forced her smile and energy, if she had used humour to avoid having to talk?

After the Christmas holidays, she has an appointment with the investigating judge for a civil claimant interview, which will determine whether or not she will join the proceedings. Costa's modus operandi was a little different in her case. He spoke about a bicycle, not about electricity. She is the only one who remembers masturbating him. So the judge is hesitating. Would slightly different evidence weaken the case, or should she withdraw this complaint?

She hesitantly makes her way through the maze of corridors in the Palais de Justice in Paris, with its gendarmes on security duty, its rushing bailiffs, its barristers perched on high heels, its handcuffed defendants. She enters the judge's chambers: huge green plants and piles of folders, everywhere, on all the tables, and on every one of the spines, five letters: COSTA.

She must report the facts. She is more precise, thanks to her work with her psychiatrist in remembering, but there are still so many questions she is incapable of answering. Who lifted up the dress? Who pulled down the pants? Everything is so blurry after his icy look. Did he pull down his pants or take his penis out of his open fly? Why does she not remember his penis, when she can see the crocodile belt with the golden buckle so clearly? And what happened afterwards? At which point did he put his fingers into her vagina? What happened before she nodded to him over the bannisters? How much time went by?

The judge asks her what consequences the events have had on her life. She goes through a few of the jellyfish, but she has no words to describe what it is, what it does to you, year after year, to live upside down. To say nothing to her parents, to her brother and sisters, to her friends. To cut herself off from others. To smile. Cover up. Exhaust herself. Spend each day outside of herself. To feel deported, without anyone knowing anything about it.

IN THE SPRING, THE Prosecutions Office issues its findings. Thirty-five cases, including her own, have been retained to form the prosecution. Hers, because she spoke again about the crocodile skin belt with its golden buckle to the investigating judge, a belt that was mentioned by other victims in the proceedings. It all hung on a detail.

Despite the colossal work of the two investigating judges, thirty-seven other similar cases are time-barred by the statute of limitations, hacked up and dumped into a mass grave.

She will therefore appear in the Assizes Court in front of Giovanni Costa, who she learns is Italian, in his seventies, of no fixed abode, a burglar who is a regular guest in various prisons, and who is, quite possibly, a serial rapist of little girls from nice neighbourhoods. All that is missing is the deep dark forest, the seven-league boots, the dripping cutlass. And the sparkling fairy who was just passing by and gave me a tap on the head with her magic wand.

I've been incredibly lucky. When I was little, my parents listened to me and took me to the police station to report the crime. I've had the emotional and financial means to fight this for almost thirty years. I was introduced to feminist ideas and a network of supportive women. I was finally diagnosed and supported in remembering by a fabulously competent and empathetic psychiatrist. In all my tender childhood, I encountered violence only once, and, more than twenty years later, a man has been arrested and charged. My case was not closed or time-barred. I had access to a compassionate barrister who was trained in the specifics of sexual violence, who steadily supported me in asking for the reclassification of my complaint and in joining the proceedings as a civil claimant. I was a little white girl from a well-to-do neighbourhood, I will be believed, I will not be sued for defamation or judged for what I was wearing that day. Giovanni Costa is an immigrant criminal, he is neither a family man nor a public figure, he will have no peers to protect him, he will certainly be found guilty. He will be designated as a monster and exposed to public outrage.

Usually there is no ogre or fairy, and sexual paedo-criminals are charming people. Members of our family, our best friends, our neighbours, our teachers, our idols, our elites. They are so convincing in their roles of honest men, of ideal parents, of devoted professionals. In France, where nearly one out of every five children is the victim of sexual violence, very few of them are listened to or treated, and even fewer assailants are sentenced by the courts. For so many centuries, our civilisation has been founded on rape culture, male domination, and child abuse. Among our ancestors, how many beaten children, how many incest victims, how many girls in forced marriages, how many women raped night after night in the dirty secrets of conjugal duty? How many husbands, how many fathers took upon themselves the right to calm their nerves with an iron rod? All human-kind is a child of rape, a frozen child, alone on the ice floe, waiting for us.

ONE SUNNY SUNDAY, SHE is sitting in the park with her brother. They're watching their children play, and her heart is overflowing with words she was never able to say, "Dear brother, I was so unhappy, I couldn't understand why, I was angry at you, at all of you, I was so angry I wanted to hurt you, I wanted to break the frame of the pretty family photograph, I wanted to chip away at your smiles, but today I understand, it's taken a while, but I understand, it wasn't you, it was him, and today, everything is possible once again, maybe I will have a new life, a whole life, a chosen life. Dear brother, in my outbursts, my nastiness, my anger, my absences, I never stopped, always, loving you all." She writes these words on paper serviettes, in notebooks, on the end-papers of books, and she notices that these scattered jottings start weaving together a rough fabric, a canvas she starts to dream about. A book? She takes advantage of every free hour, she makes the most of her commutes, of the baby's naps, of calm evenings, she reads accounts of lives torn to shreds, articles and essays about sexual violence, she cheers herself on, she takes notes, marks up her reading with pretty multi-coloured tabs, she moves a little further away from the shore and works, in the hollows of the waves, at distinguishing between the jellyfish and plastic bags. At some hours of the day, the jellyfish swarm until they invade her completely with sperm and tears, and during those hours, she can't do a thing, she knows she mustn't stay alone, so she drifts from street to street, and on the good advice of Virginia Woolf, she at last allows herself a room of her own, a table in an office where some friends work. There she finds she can be efficient, writing up workshop reports in a few hours, which might otherwise have taken her two days. She has no more time to lose, at thirty-four years of age, she needs to take the time to write.

Encouraged by her psychiatrist, she publishes a first text on the internet about the fight against sexual violence. She doesn't dare put her own name to it. She relates her experience of what trauma specialists call colonisation: the loathsome images, the violent and malignant thoughts that break and enter her mind, the hideous behaviours. She describes the blank hours, the cursed hours, those hours that victims feel so guilty about and never speak of.

After many hesitations and U-turns, she gives the text to her husband to read, and her shaking hand finds his, full of confidence.

A FEW DAYS AFTER the summer solstice, she arrives at a session with her psychiatrist feeling discouraged. The previous day, the grimacing cohort of old demons entered her heart again without warning and left her ransacked, on her knees, steaming with their filth. The psychiatrist listens to her and talks to her again about traumatic amnesia, which is so frequent with raped children. "Maybe there was something else besides his fingers in you, maybe there is still some traumatic memory trapped in the little structure of your brain called the cerebral amygdala?" She listens to her talk, but she can't follow, her jaws are so sore

a rotten stench grabs her by the nose
invades her mouth her throat
vomiting, expectorating, spewing
his cock
his cock on my lips his cock in my mouth
in my throat
his cock

He looked into my naked childhood eyes then stuck his penis into my poor smile and into the back of my throat. He suffocated me with his cock. The sore jaws, the coughing fits, the sudden choking sensations, the hatred of fellatio and the smell of men's genitals, the murderous urges when men push down on the top of my head to force my mouth around their penis, the brutal terror when I make myself vomit, the hideous images after my baby boy's birth, it suddenly all makes sense, each element falls into place and I also find my own place in this world, which is slowly straightening itself out, or maybe it's me who is suddenly standing right side up.

A few minutes, when his big penis forced its way into my tiny mouth, a few minutes found again, and with them, the full possession of my past, a coherent present, and a possible future. No more shuffling on the spot.

AT THE BEGINNING OF the summer, out in the countryside in the warm air saturated with green, sitting in the shade on two little wooden stools, my mother and I are picking black and red currants. I hadn't planned anything, hadn't premeditated it when, in the middle of an ordinary, everyday sentence, these words slip out, "Maman, he put his penis in my mouth too."

Those words, I pronounce them as if they didn't belong to me, as if I was passing the time of day, talking about war in a distant country, and she receives them, nods, murmurs, "my darling", and our hands come and go, our fingers delicately grasp the red and the black berries, our hands hadn't stopped, they keep picking and we talk about something else.

On the evening of a beautiful autumn day, a few streets away from the restaurant where I am having dinner with my husband, people are being assassinated.

In the newspapers, the monotonous past of the terrorists forms a hideous contrast with the fertile lives full of promise of each of the victims, living and dead. Nothing grows out of hate except hate itself. I cry, I shake, I scream, I read, I hope. Could the significant number of articles about the survivors' P.T.S.D. and the incredible shortage of trauma specialists in France lead to the birth of a few vocations, lead a few judges to ask themselves questions, lead to the training of a few more doctors?

And so, since I might be dead tomorrow and life is flying by, I sit myself down at my desk. I reread my sky blue notebooks, my navy blue notebooks, my red notebooks and travel diaries. They are my ropes down into the deep waters, where the daily turbulence, breathlessness, bumps, fractures, tight throat and vanishing desire, where the legion of tiny shadows will let me tell you, write you, describe you, you and the jellyfish, you whose name and face I'm not quite sure of yet. But your smell, yes, among thousands of others. And even if my nose is running or rebelling, I can still sense it so strongly when you are there, down there, in the deep, in the very depths, somewhere under there.

One morning, we're chatting in the office. The conversation bounces around as we sip our coffees and I talk about a subject close to my heart: removing the statute of limitations on sex crimes, including mass crimes, unpunished crimes, and crimes with delayed effects. I mention traumatic memory and amnesia in passing.

"How does traumatic memory work anyway?"

I love explaining things, I'm always sharing my epiphanies with others, so off I go: "Well, if you can keep these three areas of the brain in mind, the amygdala, the prefrontal cortex and the hippocampus, it's pretty simple, really."

I grab a felt-tip pen and I draw a little almond on the big whiteboard, "that's the amygdala", then a big oval, "that's the prefrontal cortex", and then a seahorse, "and that's the hippocampus.

"If something serious happens to you, the amygdala will be the first to sound the alarm and activate your fight-or-flight response to allow you to react immediately. Let's say it's a car accident, BANG. The motor is in flames, your amygdala is going to get your body to secrete adrenaline and all the other endogenous hard drugs you need so you can, let's say, get out of the car, run fifty metres, and sit down.

"Once you're safe, your prefrontal cortex will have had the time to analyse the situation, your hippocampus will have compared it with its database, and together the two of them will modulate, refine, and maybe even switch off the emotional response of the amygdala." I draw two lines that connect them to it. "Then you will realise that your ribs are really sore and that if you are seeing red, it's because your eyebrow is dripping with blood. You will think of lying down, to press a hand to the wound, to get your phone out and call 999, and your hippocampus will even allow you to tell the emergency services where you are. Then, days will go by and this memory will be stored by the hippocampus in your autobiographical memory, and it will become one of those exciting stories you tell at dinner parties.

"On the other hand, if you are a victim of rape, if you are in the presence of someone who intends to destroy you, to annihilate you, to reduce you to an object, the prefrontal cortex will search in vain, it won't be able to analyse the situation. This situation makes no sense, you are not an object. And the hippocampus can turn its archives upside down, it won't find an appropriate response to the hate it is faced with. And so, since the prefrontal cortex can't modulate or control the amygdala, and the overload of the amygdala represents a vital risk for your body, the prefrontal cortex will at least stop you from dying from an overdose of adrenaline and other endogenous drugs by breaking the circuit to disconnect the amygdala." I erase the lines connecting them, I isolate the amygdala with a solid bar.

"The amygdala is going to continue to sound the alarm, to register everything that is happening, your terror, your pain, his violence, his hatred, his perversity, but your house is empty, your cortex is unemployed, it's as if you are standing a few steps away, an idle bystander, frozen, dissociated from yourself. The trauma continues, but you feel no more emotion, no more physical pain, no more psychological pain. The hippocampus doesn't receive the necessary information anymore either, it can't file this event in your autobiographical memory, or tell you where you are in time and space. You will not consciously remember part or all of that day, the memories you will have will be confused, disorderly, as if they were unreal.

"Your emotions and the assailant's are then going to be trapped together, as they were, in your amygdala's traumatic memory, a memory with no logic, no reference points, a primitive emotional memory.

"Later on, when you're feeling better, all it will take is a smell, a sound, a word, one of the thousand and one buried fragments of the scene, one of the thousand and one triggers, for that memory to explode and invade you with thoughts of hatred and terror. You will not understand where these images come from, this violence, this horrible behaviour you inflict upon yourself. You will try to stop suffering, to stop feeling anything. You will find false comfort in bulimia, anorexia, compulsive masturbation, violent sexuality, pornography, drugs, self-harm, risk behaviours, whatever, you will find a safe place in dissociative behaviour. And that way, you will increase your stress levels so you can secrete enough endogenous hard drugs to anaesthetise yourself.

"Or else, rather than destroying yourself, you might choose to destroy others, you'll prefer the terrible efficiency of hatred as a means of dissociating. It will be your turn to become a torturer, you will anaesthetise yourself by perpetuating horrors similar to those you experienced, each time betraying the child victim you were a little more, getting high on the abuse of power, on acted-out hatred, and on lies, so as not to have to confront your despair."

Assailants are cowards. I cannot understand our fascination with the guilty parties. Rather than writing novels, television series and sensational programmes about the lives of criminals, rather than turning them into monsters to reassure ourselves of our own humanity, we should raise statues at every street corner, write biographies and screenplays, compose songs, have parades and holidays to celebrate the courage of the hundreds of millions of victims to whom no-one ever listened and who manage to make it to the end of the day alive, feeling so abandoned, so downtrodden, and so terribly alone.

THE TRIAL IS SET down for the beginning of spring. Another season to wait, sitting on the naked corner of a step, one last season, one last winter.

Session after session, securely roped up to my psychiatrist, I'm scaling my way up towards an unexpected word: recovery. I bring blurry instants and moments of gloom into the consulting room; my shadows are trail markers, signs of buried memories, memories to be exhumed, to be defused.

My conviction that I am always the last choice, a disappointment.

"The other little girl in your building, the one he talked about, was she O.K.?"

"We didn't know each other very well, she wasn't chatty, but I remember that her mother looked a bit strange and her father intimidated me."

"Her father may have been violent. Your assailant had carefully chosen that girl. It's quicker, less dangerous and even less tiring to assault someone who has already experienced violence. A victim who hasn't had any therapy dissociates herself almost immediately, assailants know how to identify them, know they won't put up a fight, and that they won't be able to say anything afterwards. The fact that you were doing fine, that you lived in a close-knit, loving family, where there was no domestic violence or corporal punishment, meant that he had to make more of an effort to make you dissociate. That's certainly why he went so far with you. To guarantee his impunity."

"So afterwards, I was easier prey than others? Is that why I attract all the perverts for miles around?"

"Yes. Unfortunately, the main risk factor in being the victim of violence is to have already experienced it. But you are recovering."

The excruciating pain in my jaws whenever I eat with pleasure.

his voice, buried, just as it was
under his dirty penis in my mouth
You like that, don't you, you're a greedy girl, aren't you.

My revulsion as soon as a lover strokes my anus
his fingers pressed
his big man's fingers opening my buttocks
my stiff body

                    his fingers fumbling his fingers forcing
                                        his fingers
                                        inside me

Not a single orifice you didn't soil. The words "rape
of a minor" weren't enough for you, you wanted to be
certain that I wouldn't talk, so you called up every single
member of the firing squad, "by vaginal, oral, and anal
penetration".

As one session follows another, the walls move back and
I discover how immense love can be, when one trusts
oneself a little more. Of course, my security guard is
still on duty, and every time I embrace my little boy,
every time I change him, or wash him, I methodically
check each one of my thoughts, but there is nothing
dirty to muddy the clear water anymore, the hideous
images don't come to disfigure my laughter, my kisses,
my tenderness.

As soon as I have a moment, I write. Often, when I'm
settled down at my desk, working, the ground suddenly
falls away, I sway, I curl up in my chair. When the crashing subsides, and I'm still astounded by the force of the
wave, I gently rub the tender skin underneath my left
wrist, all red and wet with saliva, marked by the tiny
even rectangles that my teeth left there. No-one heard
me scream, my terrors are discreet, but from now on,
even in the worst of the storms, my eyes are open wide,

and forms take shape under the sea foam, a few enormous, majestic jellyfish draw near, reaching their silky filaments out to me so I can braid them. Then I become one myself, I am Medusa, grand-daughter of the Earth and Sea, raped by Poseidon in the secret of a temple, I am innocence profaned, condemned as guilty and sentenced to see my long hair transformed into serpents, I am the one whose gaze is said to petrify anyone who sees me, I am the wild woman forced to hide in a wet cave, I am the one whose head is cut off while she is sleeping, the one whose mutilated remains terrify armies, I am what is left of a woman after she has been raped. And writing reassembles me, reconnects me, restores me.

TWO MONTHS BEFORE THE trial, I balk at going to my barrister's chambers to read the "Court Orders regarding reclassifications, partial dismissals and indictment". I end up dragging myself there by the scruff of my own neck.

First, a summary of the case and the investigation, then, for each of the victims, the established facts. After two, three, four, five terrible and similar stories, I can't read anymore, my vision is blurry, I feel dizzy, so I clutch at the names of the streets of my childhood. The street my primary school was on, rue de la Pompe; the one with my middle school, rue de la Tour; my paediatrician's, boulevard Émile-Augier; the stadium, boulevard Lannes; where my friends lived, rue Raynouard, avenue Victor-Hugo, boulevard Flandrin, rue Eugène-Manuel; the ones I often took, sometimes every day I went to school, rue Scheffer, rue Chernoviz, rue Louis-David, rue Lekain, rue Vineuse, avenue Raymond-Poincaré; the ones near my mother's office, rue Saint-Simon, rue du

Bac; the places where I used to play sometimes, square Lamartine, parc Monceau.

You were a regular, you knew the courtyards behind the buildings, the service stairs, the quiet floors. Year after year, you came to the same streets in the same neighbourhoods. Many of the victims reported seeing you again a few days, or a few months, later. One of them saw you again in the inner courtyard of her building, you saw her, you waved at her. You were so sure of yourself. Even when a few alert mothers called the police every time they found their daughter petrified by having seen you again, the officers always arrived too late.

One year after you raped me, I was walking home and, on rue Scheffer, a man called out from the opposite pavement. His wife was pregnant, he needed help to take his bags up the service stairs. My heart froze, my body turned into an automaton, I did not turn my head, I did not look at the man, I concentrated, left, right, I continued walking, left, right, I pretended not to have heard, I didn't want anything to do with those words, those words were not for me, left, right, there was a mistake. That man, that was you, Giovanni, wasn't it?

THE TRIAL IS IN three weeks and my blown-up face is back to the shape it was during my feeding-frenzy days. Seven extra kilos in a few months.

One night, I go see a play in which a friend is performing. I arrive early and drink a glass of red wine in the packed theatre foyer. A few steps away is an actress I knew at E.S.A.D., when I was in my twenties. She is radiant, wearing an elegant long blue stole and pretty brown ankle boots. I hide behind a post, I feel too much like death that evening, I don't have the strength to pretend, to smile, to answer all the "How are you"s, all the "And what about you, what are you working on at the moment? Have you been in anything lately"s.

I wish I wouldn't panic anymore when I see a familiar and friendly face, not lower my eyes, not pretend not to have seen anything. No-one has any idea how I have to haul myself up just to be able to speak, how impossible that is some days. I still feel so unworthy of them all.

All those years ruled by shame, by avoidance, by defiance, I missed so many opportunities, I aborted so many encounters and censored so many desires that, if I gave each of them a little white cross, my life would look like a vast military cemetery.

The play starts, I am sitting in the first row, the actors are amazing and suddenly a woman soars, dances, her body burns and my heart is heavy, my face awash with tears, I curl up on my seat.

At the end of the show, I feel happy about this wonderful theatrical adventure my friend is starting, and, as usual, joy carries me towards others: I dare to say hello to the woman I saw before the show. She exclaims, sincerely, "Adélaïde, you are just as beautiful as ever!" What a chasm between us. I live so little in the face she sees. I blush, say thank you, try to accept the compliment.

One day in May, my eyes, which had seen so little until then, looked helplessly at a man's face twisting, contorting, emptying itself of all its humanity. That day, I registered in the most intimate depths of my being Ugliness, Abjection, Evil. More Evil than I could ever understand. It lasted a long time, didn't it Giovanni? Your face is still hiding inside me, that's what I catch sight of every day under my tired features, my cellulite and my sagging tummy.

In a few weeks, you will be there. I hope that seeing

you will expel the face I saw that day from me. I hope I will be able to get rid of your features, at last, and stop confusing them with mine.

THE TRIAL STARTS IN two weeks and is expected to last eight days. I don't know if my father or my brother and sisters know about it. I mentioned it a couple of times to my mother. It's almost always me who talks about it, and so little. They don't know what happened in our stairwell that day. They have heard me say that my request for reclassification to "rape" had been success- ful, that I was joining the proceedings as a civil claimant, and that I was trying to write a book about it.

My girlfriends offer to come and support me, but the people I really want by my side are my parents, my brother, my sisters. I am lucky that a man has been arrested, that there are other victims to corroborate my statements, that my mother remembers, that the law believes me, and I would like to grab hold of that luck like a megaphone, to say to my brother and sisters, my parents, "Look at me, for years I carried hatred, terror, violence, ugliness. Look, they did not belong to me, but to him, the man in the dock. For years now, you and

I have hardly known each other except through my excesses, our silences. Look, here I am in front of you today, naked, here is my injured body, my damaged body, look at me, I need to be able to fall into your arms at last, I need you to be there to stand together with me."

I take the opportunity of an email exchange to give them the dates of the court proceedings, and to suggest they come meet me at the Palais de Justice at lunchtime. Only one of my sisters answers, the one who knows, from her own experience, the unimaginable depth of the impact. She has blocked out three days to come and support me.

A few days later, helped by a glass of wine or two, I talk to a cousin about it at a party one evening. He listens to me, supports me, encourages me. For him, for my sister, I would like to weave a crown of palm leaves and parade them in triumph on a chariot full of flowers through the jubilant city.

And so, at the next family Sunday lunch, I have courage in my heart and only one goal in mind, to say: "It's going to be tough, I need you." Just so I don't later regret not having asked them.

Sitting at the big table, I'm waiting for someone to throw me a line, to reply to my suggestion of lunch, to ask for details about the court case, which we have never talked about, to show concern. They talk about the arrangements for the next holidays, who's going where,

the American elections, the children, the meal is whiz-
zing past and I don't manage to say the words, I smile at
everyone, I pass the dishes, I slice the tarts, and suddenly,
a quiet moment, I say "right, now", but in the time it
takes for me to be afraid, someone has already started
talking about something else, and the children are coming and going, coffee in the living room, all the little
side conversations, then they all get up and get ready
to leave, there are tears in my eyes, I bite my tongue, I
frantically look for my jumper, my sister-in-law, at the
door, asks "What about your court case?"

I manage to say, "it's going to be tough", and run
back to the dining room to have a cry, then I open my
eyes wide, pinch my cheeks, come back with a big smile,
we say good-bye too, and take the lift. As soon as I get
outside, I burst into sobs.

I needed love and comfort so badly. I hate myself for
not being able to ask, I hate them for not seeing it, or
not having dared.

A few days later, my mother calls. She will be there,
my father too, they will take turns to be at my side, and
she offers to call my brother and sisters to organise a
roster.

The storm dies down inside me, and through the transparent blue, I can see the ocean floor.

*

I was afraid of my father's silence. I write to him, "Maman tells me that you will try to come, I can't imagine how difficult it must be for a father to talk about these kinds of things with his daughter, but here we are, I would be very touched if you both came along, I need you, I will need my Papa's arms." Simple words, and yet, it had taken me years to be able to say them.

Beyond all hope, all of them will come, my husband, my mother, my father, my sisters, my brother, my aunts, my cousins. Every day, the veil that separated us will tear a little more, I will let myself be taken into their arms and in our furtive embraces so many words will no longer be necessary.

My girlfriends will also be there – those who can, those who won't break down at seeing me fall apart.

And all of them will be there to stand together with me.

III

FIRST DAY OF PROCEEDINGS. I prepared my armour last night with care, flattering, discreet, comfortable clothes, I washed my hair, waxed and moisturised my legs. I have a date with myself.

The air outside is heavy with a coming storm, I hurry on my bike between last night's puddles, my eyes stinging, my heart ready. The streets are empty. In front of a high school, an ingenious pyramid of green rubbish bins announces the impending strike action against the new labour law. As soon as I get to the île de la Cité, the downpour starts, I lock my bike to a railing, I run into the café where I find my mother with her worried smile. I take a deep breath in, I breathe out in hurried little staccato breaths, I stare at the other women at the bar. Which ones are the other victims? Having gulped down our coffee, we cross the boulevard du Palais, pass the security gates, the vast stone steps, the grey solemnity of the grand hall, the K stairway, the gendarmes on duty. I enter the Victor Hugo courtroom.

The room is panelled in dark wood, with a blue-grey

ceiling crowded with plaster symbols, and alcoves along the side walls. On the right, these alcoves enclose large windows looking out onto the stone steps, the high gates, the boulevard du Palais. On the left, one of them contains the dock, enclosed by wooden and tinted glass panels. Giovanni Costa will be seated there, in a while, and from that platform he will face the benches for the civil claimants. He will only see our profiles, unless we choose to turn towards him. Beside him the Court Registrar, whose desk takes up the end of the wide arc where the jurors will sit, with the Président, the Presiding Judge, in the centre, and his two Assessor Judges at his sides. At the other end, the desk of the Prosecutor, the Avocat Général, and the little table of the Court Bailiff. Then, on either side of the central aisle, heavy polished wooden benches, on the left for the Defence, on the right for the Prosecution. At the back, a long railing behind which three narrow rows of chairs are filling up. In the centre, the witness stand. A miniscule wood and brass box, polished like a ship's wheel by all the hands that have clutched it, the focal point of the court. That's where you swear to speak without hate or fear, to tell the whole truth and nothing but the truth. There, words have weight, words determine the course of whole lives.

The room is rustling with conversations and coats piled up on laps. There are lots of us victims here, I say to myself, and lots of people supporting us.

Giovanni Costa steps into the dock. I stare at him, but I don't recognise him, I don't recognise anything of the man in the month of May in this dishevelled old geezer, nylon tracksuit jacket and tired T-shirt, sunken eyes and bald skull ringed with grey hair, I don't recognise him, this paunchy man struggling to sit down, I'm staring at him though, I can't tear my eyes away, suddenly his eyes are animated and from his perch, he is scrutinising all of us in the courtroom, methodically, one by one. My stomach aches, I'm frightened, he's looking for us, I can hardly breathe, his gaze is getting closer, I crush the hand of my psychiatrist sitting next to me, he's going to see me, I can't turn my head away. Suddenly his blows rain down on me. He has dug his hard pupils into mine and all my muscles have tensed, my body is riddled with hatred, I'm struggling to get my breath back: the man in the stairwell, the man in the month of May, the man from twenty-six years ago and every single day since, that's him. Giovanni Costa.

As the Presiding Judge enters, the court rises and is seated in silence, and as he reads out the twenty-four names of those summoned for jury duty in this session of the Assizes Court, I gradually realise that the people in the audience are not the victims and their supporters, no, these are the random people whose fate it may be to determine ours.

A few challenges later, the courtroom is nearly empty.

Six jurors take their seats alongside the Presiding Judge. A handsome thirty-something man with a clipped beard. A man with a chubby face and a tender gaze. A tired old man. An elegant woman with a fresh shampoo and set. Charles Berling's double. A woman with lively eyes behind round glasses.

Four alternate jurors. A dignified, well-dressed young man. A little old lady with white hair held back by a wide black headband. A dynamic young retired woman. A woman with a round face framed with brown hair.

The Presiding Judge is entirely at ease with his long red gown and his Judge's face on, he speaks calmly with affable, carefully chosen words.

The Prosecutor is huge, short salt-and-pepper beard and tortoiseshell glasses.

Since the barrister who assisted Giovanni Costa during the investigation has withdrawn from the case, two Secrétaires de la Conférence are assigned to him, young barristers who have won the annual eloquence prize, and are therefore appointed to represent defendants with no counsel. They will not have had much time to take stock of their client, even if the one thousand seven hundred and ninety-four pages of the Costa brief fit onto a U.S.B. flashdrive. As soon as the Presiding Judge calls their names, Costa stands up and rejects them. The

Presiding Judge informs him that, at the Assizes Court, even though he does have the right to ask his barristers to be silent, he does not have the right to self-representation. Costa makes an off-colour joke about "beautiful women". I find it hard to understand him, he speaks with a strong Italian accent.

When their names are read out, a few victims called as witnesses stand up, and then leave. When no-one is there to answer a name, the Presiding Judge says "pass", more and more perplexedly, as the list of absentees grows longer and longer. Rhythmic sounds of whistles and slogans come in from the long march of protesters outside on the boulevard. Sitting in silence on the benches for civil claimants, there are two of us, a young woman with angular contours and a soft gaze, and me.

Giovanni Costa reigns.

The Presiding Judge starts to read the list of charges to the court, and at the second item, "Having, in Paris, on May 13, 1990, in any event on national territory and in a period not time-barred by the statute of limitations, through violence, constraint, threat or surprise, committed an act of sexual penetration on the person of Adélaïde Bon, in this case notably by introducing a finger into the vagina of the victim, with the circumstance that these acts were committed on a minor of less than fifteen years, born on March 1, 1981", at the second item Costa jumps

up, with his hands gripping the tinted glass, and howls:
"You're the one who rapes little girls, you Nazi!"

I am in the stairwell in my building
terrified
paralysed
I can't breathe anymore

"Monsieur Costa, you may speak later."

"Go fuck yourself, you child rapist, it's all lies, I'm not a rapist!"

"Monsieur Costa."

"You're talking shit, get fucked!"

"Monsieur Costa."

"No-one is here! Where are the victims? Where are the civil claimants? Get fucked!"

"Monsieur Costa, I am asking you to calm down."

"Where are the witnesses? Arsehole!"

"Monsieur Costa, calm down, otherwise I will have to exclude you from deliberations for the day."

"Where are they, arsehole? You bastard! You Italian slave! Where are they?"

He is taken out of the dock by two gendarmes. My body shatters.

As calm returns, the Presiding Judge continues his reading of the martyrology. I don't hear any of it, I'm sobbing.

*

Now that the judge has named the crime, the accused has revealed some of his habitual violence, and the victim is wracked with ancient sobs, everyone is here in their rightful place.

After the lunch break, a policeman from the Paris Minors' Protection Unit is called to give evidence. It's the captain who called me, one winter evening, three years ago, and who interviewed me a few months later.

At the Assizes Court, the proceedings are oral, the Presiding Judge is the only member of the jury who is acquainted with the facts and circumstances of the case, so the policeman tells the jurors and Assessor Judges about the long course of the investigation that resulted in the arrest of "the electrician". He has the muted voice of someone who doesn't like public speaking, and everyone is straining to hear him better.

Approximately twenty reports of rape, attempted rape and sexual assault on minors between 1983 and 1984.

Approximately twenty reports of rape, attempted rape and sexual assault on minors between 1990 and 1991.

Approximately thirty reports of rape, attempted rape and sexual assault on minors between 1994 and 2003.

Almost all of them committed in the western districts of Paris, by a balding man with a singsong voice, a middle-aged man who asks for help from little girls.

Often his pretext is a light bulb, a fuse box, a meter box. He manipulates their soft little hearts, isolates them, pretends to give them a leg up and stuffs his mitts between their thighs, takes off their clothes, feels their nipples, rubs his penis against their vulvas, their buttocks, slaps them if they cry, penetrates them with his fingers, with his penis, sometimes ejaculates on their clothes.

Four little girls are taken to the forensic medical emergency services and their clothes, soiled with sperm, are placed in sealed storage in the police archives.

From 1990 to 1993, a first judicial investigation leads to a dismissal, the perpetrator is not identified.

From 1996 to 1998, the Minors' Unit assembles fifty-six similar claims in a synthesis report about the so-called "electrician". A second judicial investigation leads to a dismissal, the perpetrator is not identified.

In 2001, a suspect is arrested. From the clothes in sealed storage (three pairs of white cotton pants, one pair of jogging trousers, one grey T-shirt) the forensic police extract traces of D.N.A. from a single individual. Who is not the arrested suspect.

From 2002 to 2005, a third judicial investigation leads to a dismissal, the perpetrator is not identified. The case is closed. End of story.

But then, along comes a lithe and resolute woman, an investigator from the Crimes Unit who is in it for the long haul, and who decides to devote part of her retirement to reopening unresolved matters, so-called cold cases. And she chooses to exhume the case of "the electrician". After searching like a worker bee and making hundreds of telephone calls, she manages to locate the various pieces of evidence stored under seals and, since science has made some progress, in 2010, she obtains permission from the Prosecutions Office for the establishment of a more precise genotype.

It is thanks to this heroine from the shadows, whose name I don't even know, and thanks to the series of teams that conserved the evidence, that at the start of 2011, the D.N.A. of the electrician is registered in the National Automated D.N.A. Database, the one so dear to my high-school friend Sigrid's father.

In April 2012, after a neighbourhood brawl, a certain Giovanni Costa is taken into custody. His police record reveals a past with numerous convictions for burglary, so the diligent police officer takes a sample of his D.N.A. to enter it into the database. In May, it appears that this D.N.A. matches that of "the electrician".

In June, the third judicial investigation is reopened, the investigators need to find the original police reports, locate and re-interview the numerous victims, and arrest Giovanni Costa.

He is apprehended in October, sitting at a bus stop, not far from the second-hand shops he usually deals with, sitting where he has been in the habit of sitting for years, where those who know him have always been sure of finding him. He is not a man in hiding.

As soon as he is arrested, Giovanni Costa rejects the claims, denies the presence of D.N.A., cries that there is a conspiracy hatched against him by the Italian police and African dealers, showers everyone, especially the women, with insults, claims that he has a double, that there is nothing wrong with seducing French whores, that he is an Italian stallion who all women fight over.

The captain concludes: "In the course of my twenty-year career with the Minors' Unit, I have never had to deal with such an individual."

The police inspector who gives evidence next tells the court about an interrogation. "We spread photographs of little girls on the table, and he becomes enraged, 'I am not a rapist, the sperm on their pants, it's the father's or the grandfather's, ask them, it's a statistical certainty!' He throws all the photos off the table, and screams at me, 'you slut, you let all the dogs fuck you', he pulls out the cables from the computer that has been recording everything."

None of the reported incidents took place during his numerous prison terms for burglaries.

When he talks about his "trade", stealing, he describes a modus operandi that corresponds on all points with the accounts of the little victims. "I would pretend I was an electricity or gas repairman. I would just wait quietly at the bottom of a building for someone to go in, to get to the service stairs. Once inside, I would say I had come to adjust an appliance. I would show them to the meter box, if there was no step ladder, I'd give them a leg up, I told them to check that the numbers were changing over. In the meantime, I would go into the bedroom, take whatever was there, especially jewellery, and then leave."

The genetic profile from the four items of clothing matches his, a profile whose frequency in the general population is less than one in seven billion.

The inspector's voice resounds through the silent court-room as she adds, "In ten years at the Minors' Unit, I've seen my share of sexual predators. Not one of them affected me like he did, because of the sheer number of his victims, and because he had absolutely no considera-tion for them, or anyone else. In my experience, nobody becomes a sexual paedo-criminal at fifty years old. Violence allows him to escape any questions."

What was Giovanni Costa's life, over his seventy-eight years? No-one knows anything about it, or only very little.

He was born in 1938, at Villa Rosa, a little town in Sicily, into a practicing Catholic family. Of this family, "he has not seen anyone since he left, in 1958," his sister-in-law assured the carabinieri. He phoned her in 1989, when he had no money to pay for a lawyer for one of his numerous incarcerations. His sister-in-law then transferred a few pennies every month from the estate of his father, who had died two years previously and made his son's inheritance conditional on his coming to the funeral. Once the inheritance was spent, he never contacted her again.

Only his police record gives a little information about his comings and goings:

Between the age of twenty and twenty-nine, he is in Belgium, visiting courts and prisons. He is convicted six times in Charleroi, Liège and Brussels for robbery, attempted robbery, receiving stolen goods, assault and battery, identity fraud, forgery and falsification of documents.

He is thirty-one years old, in France, convicted in Marseille for theft and possession of a weapon, then in Saint-Ouen for receiving stolen goods, theft and possession of a weapon. He spends six months in prison, gets out for a few months, is arrested again for attempted robbery in Paris, then in Colombes. After one of many offences leading to a deportation order and a refusal of entry or stay in French territory, at La Queue-en-Brie, he assumes various identities, such as that of Salvatore Trapani, a school classmate who had emigrated to the United States.

He is forty-one years old, arrested in Paris for aggravated robbery. He spends a year in prison. Two Parisian convictions later, two more years in prison, for aggravated robbery, receiving stolen goods, forgery of an official document, offences leading to a deportation order. No sooner is he out than he is back in again, at forty-nine, sentenced in Paris to four years in prison for robbery, etc. He is granted conditional release less than two years later.

He is fifty-four, sentenced in Paris to four years in prison for similar offences. He is again granted conditional release less than two years later.

He is sixty-six, convicted in Paris for aggravated robbery, unlawful possession of a weapon, forgery and falsification of documents.

He is seventy-four, convicted in Paris for assault with a weapon and concealing evidence. This time, while in custody, a diligent officer takes a small sample of his D.N.A.

How life repeats itself for those who persist in trying to destroy it.

The police investigator who is called to give evidence about his personality and life story goes no further than summarising what he told her during their prison interviews: she wasn't able to verify anything of his long, ranting accounts. "He was never employed, he said he worked under the table in hospitality and cabinet-making, studied law in Switzerland in 1957. He said he lived in London, between 1972 and 1974, and that he steals only from rich people. He mostly lived in hotels. He has balls of steel. He claims to have stayed with the same woman for fourteen years, but cannot remember even her first name. He is passionate about horse racing, prostitutes, and shoes, especially crocodile skin shoes. He boasted about having bought dozens of pairs, in the good years, and he always took great care to have perfectly pedicured feet (at the time of his arrest, he had a complete pedicure set on him). He claims the rapist is his doppelganger, but he still doesn't provide any alibis, he can't remember where he was on the days of the events, he travels so much. Oh, except for one of the victims whose pants were stained with his D.N.A., he says 'that's all lies', that day he was watching the football World Cup final between Italy and Brazil at the Worringer Hotel in Düsseldorf (a final that took place the following month). He says he is a burglar not a rapist, he was well brought-up, he is Italian, desirable, virile, a stallion, a man, a real one."

She finishes with, "I think he also wanted to use me to contact the Investigating Judge."

The young woman sitting with me on the benches for civil claimants is called to the witness box. The Presiding Judge projects a photograph of her face as a child onto the screens. It's her birthday, a few months before the rape, and behind the candles and the chocolate cake decorated with Smarties, a little girl with her fringe in a mess is looking back at us, winking, smiling with all her teeth. And here she is, years later, standing very straight, her hands clutching the railing of the witness box. She tells the story, with no digressions or pathos, of her dark day and survival afterwards. When she stands down, we clasp hands with guarded fervour.

The Presiding Judge then reads out the witness statement of an absent victim: one of the two girls whose names I recognised in the Witness Notification, the one who was in middle school with me. The Judge reads out the barbarous facts, and I think of that plump, timid girl, with her kind eyes, whom I often saw but hardly knew. I hope she had someone to hold her hand.

After the twenty-four times he said "pass" that morning, the forward-thinking Presiding Judge cancels a full day of proceedings, since reading statements takes much less time than hearing the halting evidence – often interrupted by long periods of silence – of the witnesses in the box.

That evening, with knots in my stomach, I prepare to give evidence the following day. Meanwhile the men and women of France prepare for their first *Nuit Debout*: a night they spend standing on the place de la République, which has become a catafalque for the victims of one terrorist attack after another. Those men and women give back to the statues on the square, buried in snuffed candles and soaked memorial posters, the lustre of their allegories: *Liberté, Egalité, Solidarité.*

THE SECOND DAY. A new young woman, whose body is so tense it looks as though it might shatter, is sitting trembling beside me. Giovanni Costa is observing us. As soon as she comes forward to give evidence, he snorts, as soon as she opens her lips, he insults the Presiding Judge. "Get fucked", etc. And again, he is excluded from the proceedings for the day.

It's my turn to give evidence. I step forwards shakily, feeling disappointed. I would have liked him to be sitting in the dock as I stand in the witness box, I would have liked him to hear me, I would have liked it to be my turn to talk and his turn to be quiet, I would have liked to tell him the details of each of my wounds, I would have liked the Presiding Judge to order him to account for them.

That afternoon, as is my right as a civil claimant, I have called my psychiatrist, Dr Salmona, to appear as an expert witness.

Alive with passion and competence, with the simplicity that belongs to great souls, she explains, precisely, medically, backed up by scientific studies, what it means to live a whole life after a rape.

After her presentation, the jurors, the Presiding Judge, the Prosecutor, all ask questions.

"Please excuse this technical question, but for it to be a rape, does the hymen have to be ruptured?"

"Absolutely not. The hymen is a permeable membrane, and in two thirds of child rapes, no ruptures are apparent."

"Is it really possible to forget that one has been raped?"

"Yes, and sometimes for decades. The majority of children who are victims of sexual violence present with complete or partial traumatic amnesia connected to the dissociation mechanism the brain sets off to protect itself from the extreme stress generated by the violence."

"Can memories of a rape be invented or altered?"

"Absolutely not, they are not conscious autobiographical memories, memories that are situated in time and fade as the years go by, and that can be consciously brought to mind, or retold, analysed or transformed. No, traumatic memory generated by rape is different, it is outside time, it intrudes as if the event were happening again in real time, it repeats itself in the same unchanging way and with the same initial emotional charge, with the same details. Passing years have no effect on it. Like the black boxes of airplanes. Traumatic memory is involuntary, invasive, uncontrollable and undifferentiated."

"Is it possible to recover from a rape?"

"Yes, thankfully, if the victim is offered specific treatment. She will need to go through the traumatic events to integrate them into her autobiographical memory at last, but to do that she needs to be supported by someone trained in the treatment of P.T.S.D."

"Is there such a thing as sexual attraction to children?"

"No. Sex crimes against children have nothing to do with desire or sexuality. Violence generates extreme stress in the assailant, an overload of the amygdala, it sets off the same trauma mechanisms as it does in the victim. Except that he is using the victim as an antalgic, he chooses to provoke this emotional storm in order to stimulate the massive production of endogenous hard drugs and then cause a dissociation and an emotional anaesthesia. He wants to stop suffering, to feel invincible, all-powerful, and every time he commits a crime, he develops a more and more powerful addiction to extreme violence. The purer the victim, the more abject the crime is, the stronger the anaesthetic effect will be. Sexual paedo-criminals are chemically addicted to violence."

*

Since 2003, not a single report to the police. Where were you, Giovanni? What did you do to your victims, so that not a single one of them came forward?

CLARA, MARGUERITE, ADÉLAÏDE, Stéphanie, Leïla, Myriam, Sophia, Alice, Melinda, Maria, Sophie, Marie, Anna, Mathilda, Clotilde, Sybille, Juliette, Philippine, Julia. In the end there are nineteen of us who give evidence.

Fourteen civil claimants, nine of whom have joined the proceedings only a few days, a few hours, a few minutes before giving evidence, all of the witnesses telling of the days of terror preceding their appearance, all of them trembling with the determination they needed to find inside themselves to be able to speak in court.

One of the very first civil claimants to join has not made an appearance, and neither has her counsel. The Bailiff and the Registrar call her, leave messages. They contact her barrister. "She does not want to give evidence or be represented, she is terrified." Like her, thirteen young women will not appear, they will fail to answer their subpoenas, preferring to take the risk of criminal sanctions for not attending court, rather than having to break the seals on the memories of their own hideous day and its long aftermath.

On the third day of the trial, when my parents, my sisters and I are out for lunch on the place du Châtelet, I recognise one of them. I recognise her because she has famous parents and I had looked for her face on Google one solitary evening. She is waiting for someone just in front of the restaurant, waiting for quite a long time, and I want to go to her, and say, "Excuse me, you don't know me, but we were the victims of the same man. His trial is happening a few steps away from here. I just wanted to tell you, to let you know. But maybe that's why you're here, why you came back to France?" I hang on to that ridiculous hope, and don't go out to her. At this moment she looks so radiant, she seems so serene, I'm afraid my words will pour rancid hot oil on the brightness of the day.

The next day, when the Presiding Judge reads her witness statement in her absence, giving voice to the despair of this young woman who was only six years old when Costa took her, revealing the extent of the disaster and everything she had to do to survive, I have a heavy heart for not having dared to speak to her.

And there are all those victims whose cases are time-barred by the statute of limitations and whose witness statements were not sought by the court.

*

I noted down the names of those who were absent on the inside cover of my notebook, and every day of the trial, I take them in with me. Céline, Anaïs, Caroline, Constance, Anne, Sophie, Toinon, Charlotte, Aurore, Alice, Anne, Juliette, Gwendoline, Sophie, Sandra, Marine, Laura, Anaïs, Florence, Elsa, Perrine, Albane, Chloé, Victoria, Ingrid, Alicia, Raphaëlle, Véronique, Laure, Élise, Delphine, Vanessa, Saïda, Céline, Yun, Marie-Eugénie, Sandra, Claire, Amélie, Patricia, Sophie, Marie-Christine, Stéphanie, Tatiana, Adeline, Élodie, Marine.

And there are the others, all the others, the ones who were never able to make a report.

And there is you, Giovanni. You who devoted your life to robbery and rape.

"WHERE ARE THE WITNESSES? I want to see the witnesses! Just show me the girls who are accusing me! Put them in front of me! They have to come here and tell me I raped them! There has to be a meeting! Bring me the victims who are accusing me! Make just one woman stand in front of me and tell me I raped her. One! I want her to face me!" you screamed at each interrogation.

So much so that the investigating judge later refused to send you the complete file of the investigation, with the justification that "there exists a risk of pressure being put on the civil claimants and witnesses if Monsieur Costa obtained a copy of their interviews and their postal and telephone contacts".

But then on the evening of the fourth day, all the evidence of the victims registered on the Court Orders had been heard, and you were not there. You did not answer a single question, you did not submit to any cross-examination, you did not face a single one of us.

The first two days, you managed to get excluded from

the proceedings at the very beginning of the day by telling the Presiding Judge five or six times to "get fucked", and the following days you allowed yourself to be transferred from the prison to the "mousetrap" cells in the Palais de Justice, but then you refused to be taken out of them, insulting the bailiff responsible for informing you of your obligation to attend in the morning, then insulting the Registrar responsible for informing you of what had happened in the evening.

Every morning, you made us wait for more than an hour. Every evening, you obliged the Presiding Judge to beg a bailiff to come to the Palais the following morning. The proceedings cannot start until you have reiterated your refusal to attend in front of a bailiff, and in Paris there are only two such bailiffs who accept this poorly paid job.

I imagine you stewing in your hatred in a damp underground cell smelling of urine, but that doesn't make anything any better. How can I break free from you without seeing you?

A barrister reads a letter from a mother to your empty dock. "We had the courage to come and give evidence. Will you have the candour to answer us?" Your absence is your response. You give us nothing. Nothing to analyse, nothing to discuss, nothing to confront. You are above the law. This trial does not concern you. We do not exist. For you, we never existed.

*

After the first witness statement, the disappointed journalists had already deserted their stall. Without the robber-rapist of little rich girls, without the raving monster, the story lacks spice. Pain is much less exciting than hatred. The trial of some Somali pirates is taking place not far away, it will get a lot more attention than the frightening banality of raped children.

And so one by one, facing the sniggering contempt of the empty dock and the inquisitorial looks of the jury, gripping the railing of the witness box like a skiff, we set aside the pretty masks we had so patiently crafted, took down our defences, let the tears we had held back for so long flow at last, and tried to put disaster into words.

All of me is held in each of the witness statements, in each of their words. And in the mirrors that each of these women's stories holds up, I rid myself of some of your story.

I met this man when I was about ten years old and – long silence

I prefer to answer questions – she bursts into tears

After we had lunch at home, I was going back to school with my little sister, and an old man called out to me, he needed help with a light bulb in a stairwell.

Since I was sick, I stayed at home that day, someone knocked at the door, I looked through the peephole: I didn't

see anyone, I thought that the concierge had left the post on the doormat, I opened and there was a man on the stairs, he came back up when he saw me, he introduced himself as the electrician for the building, he asked me if I was home alone.

That day, I'd had an argument with my parents, I wanted to pedal fast to get home first, my bike chain fell off, a man appeared and offered to fix it if I helped him change a light bulb.

I was crossing parc Monceau, which was crowded at lunchtime, I was going to football with my brother and a gardener asked me to help him move some flowerpots, for a ten-franc piece.

He was the building caretaker, his wife was pregnant, he needed help to change a light bulb, he would give me some money.

An old man told me he was having trouble walking, he took my arm.

His wife was pregnant, he had heavy things to move.

He was an old man, I held the door for him.

A man told me his wife was pregnant and that they had no more water.

He was very embarrassed to have to ask me that.

I was a helpful child. And he promised me an ice cream.

I didn't dare say so afterwards, but he promised me a ten-franc piece.

I'm from a Catholic family, I was a girl-scout, I was trying to be helpful.

He wasn't frightening, rather pitiful.

221

I was brought up in a family where you lend a hand.
I wanted to help him repair that meter box.
I knew I wasn't supposed to talk to strangers, but he looked
so kind, so embarrassed to ask for help.
I was a docile little girl.

he looked several times in the direction of the caretaker's flat
suddenly I was very afraid
he asked my little brother to keep an eye on something
he told my friend to wait for me downstairs
he took me to the top of the service stairs
he took me to the storage area for the rubbish bins
he took me into the basement

"Follow me or I'll strangle you", I was very frightened,
I followed him

there was a grey box on the wall
I could tell it was out of service
there was a kind of window up high
there was a handle to turn
the light was working I didn't dare say anything

I remember – long silence – the look in his eyes

I was frightened he would kill me I did what he said
I was petrified with terror
I thought he's going to kill me

I have his look – she stops

he tried several times to lift me up my feet
didn't leave the ground but each time my T-shirt
would go up a bit higher he pretended to try
to carry me he squeezed my nipples harder and harder
he lifted me up several times as
his hands gradually moved to my breasts and then
– um – what happened?

he grabbed my buttocks when he lifted me up
he asked me how much I weighed then he grabbed
me by the buttocks

"You are very pretty", he licked my neck
"Can we have a kiss? I'm not going to eat you",
he kissed me on the lips
"Be nice to me", he kissed me
by force all over on my neck and my face
he told me I was beautiful and kind
he licked my cheek
"I won't eat your breasts, I'm married"
he licked my breasts
he kissed me three times
then he put his whole hand in my mouth

I managed to escape I ran down the stairs
he was laughing so loud I screamed to my little sister

to run and open the door
it was winter I was wearing several layers he gave up
trying to undress me completely I was wearing a playsuit
attached by a tie around my neck he spent some time
fussing with the knot he didn't manage to untie it

my trousers were in the way he pulled them down
little by little he said
he was allergic to denim so I had to take off my shorts
and yet my shorts weren't made of denim
he had a strange metal tool I was afraid he would
hit me with it I did as I was told and took off my knickers

suddenly I realised I was all naked, I have no idea how

I was facing him, he asked me to hold him around his neck
he held me tight against him he mimed gestures to make me
understand that if I resisted he would strangle me
he pinned me against a wall he rubbed himself against my
buttocks it was all hard inside his trousers "You're crying
over nothing, you're
just a kid. The others don't cry like that", he
opened his fly he showed me his willy he slapped me
"I don't like children who cry", he put me
on the desk I didn't have my trousers on anymore he was
rummaging
around by my vulva I was very afraid I cried lots
he punched me hard he put two fingers in

my vagina it really hurt I wanted to scream but I
couldn't get a sound out he started laughing he put his
fingers
inside he smelled them he licked them he gave a sort of
strangled
laugh it burned inside me I was asking him to stop he
slapped me
several times he was laughing making fun of me making fun
of my fear he wiggled his fingers in my vagina: "You'll feel
better after this", he hurt me very badly he started again,
"I'm
only putting my fingers in, stop crying", afterwards he was
licking his
hand and I was crying he touched my anus with his
fingers with his penis, "Stop crying or I'll give you
a spanking", he didn't manage to penetrate me with his
penis
when I was stuck to the wall so he laid me down on
the stairs he spread my legs it hurt so much
"Be quiet, people are going to think I want to rape you."

there are some details I remember very precisely and yet
it's all so confused in my head I hardly remember
anything I think I've repressed a lot of things
I think that there are a lot of things that have disappeared
from my memory
sperm was found in my pants
I couldn't remember anything I don't remember but if I

said so at the time it was certainly true I was not
the kind of girl to lie I said I saw his penis but now
I don't remember I don't know anymore – she cries –
for me it's just a void

afterwards he told me he was an honest man
that he was a father
that he had two children a boy and a girl that
his name was "Salvator, the saviour".

"You were nice to me", he took me to the
bakery to buy me the lollies he promised I was
petrified I didn't dare say anything to the shopkeeper who
knew me well he gave me four or five ten-franc
pieces he told me I had done him a favour that
deserved a reward he put a coin in my hand
he wanted to give me money ten francs twenty francs
thirty francs I refused he made me swear not to say anything
"We are friends now"

he wanted to see me again he asked me what I was doing on
Wednesday he asked me what time I finished school
he would have liked to see me again he suggested we make
a time for a rendezvous later he made me promise
to come back

he went away he left the door open I was terrified I
didn't dare leave my room I was afraid he would come back

he stayed in the neighbourhood all afternoon
he waited for me for hours at the front door of our building

Maman found me lifeless senseless
it was the neighbour on our floor who called the police
when the policemen asked me to show them what he
had touched in the apartment well he had only touched
me there were no fingerprints anywhere
he made me open all the doors all the drawers move
the stool touch the meter box

at the police station there were lots of policemen I was
terrified I didn't say much
I knew I had done something wrong that I had
followed a stranger
I didn't tell them everything
I felt guilty for holding the door open for him
I didn't tell them everything
I was ashamed I didn't tell about him touching me I was in
a hurry for the interview to end
I didn't dare talk about his erect penis and also I
had no words to express it

my father was beside himself he searched for him all over
the neighbourhood all night he took us to live
in the South the next year
it was my mother's friend who talked to the police about me
my parents were told

but they never spoke to me about it
my father was very angry with me he reproached
me for not behaving properly for not screaming
my mother was so shocked that we left
in a rush to live in a provincial town the following year a
departure with disastrous consequences for the whole family
my parents told me it was a secret
we never spoke of it again
my father told me never to tell anyone about it otherwise
they would look at me differently
I grew up as a recluse until I was twenty-one my parents
never let me leave home alone again no more
birthday parties no more class outings no more
pyjama parties no more school trips
no more anything except
sometimes McDonald's with my mother
I couldn't talk to anyone about it
even the psychotherapist
my parents took me to
at home we never talked about it again it was taboo
I had to keep everything inside me I shut
myself off from everyone I built my personality on suspicion

I felt so guilty

I told my best friend and she ridiculed me
in front of everyone
people found out in middle school someone left a message on

our answering machine at home "You shouldn't have
reported it to the police. We're going to get you bitch"
girls from my class wrote a threatening letter making
me believe it was from him

whether it had any consequences in my life?
– she shrugs, unable
to say another word
after-effects? – long silence –
I was lucky – voice breaking.
it was a huge trauma
it was a rupture it completely isolated me
it hurt me very badly later on
– she bursts into tears.
he completely destroyed me – silence.
it blocked me in everything
it wrecked my life

it's being all alone lost in the forest at night
it's a very physical sensation
that comes along all of a sudden anytime
for a long time I used to see
images of what happened to me before I went to sleep
I started sucking my thumb again
I had lots of nightmares
I'm still afraid of the dark now
I could never go out for a walk alone – she dissolves in tears –
in my neighbourhood for months I didn't dare

go to school I would see him
everywhere I could never do anything at school
I have great difficulties concentrating
it takes up all the room I found
a safe place in my studies I became anorexic
I became bulimic

I was afraid of all men even of my father
I didn't want my father to take me in his arms
it destroyed my relationship with my father he never
understood the impact it had on me

my first sexual relations? – her voice breaks,
she can no longer speak.

I still remember his fingers inside me I am terrified during
penetration I still have the sensation of his
fingers pushing between the lips of my vulva if I
have sexual intercourse with my husband it's
out of obligation I
take no pleasure in it
I put together a system of invisibility
no-one sees me
I became bulimic
so that men don't see me
I started being suspicious of everyone
it's better not to be too kind in life
I find it very hard to trust anyone

especially men I tend to freeze
and not be able to say no I'm always afraid
of losing control with men
I'm very suspicious I can't stand being alone
in an enclosed space with a man who has any
authority over me so taking driving lessons
going to the doctor being in my boss'
office I just can't stand it

I am so emotional since then that I
often lose consciousness
I constantly live in fear
I think about it all the time it's like a cloud
inside my head
I feel abnormal, broken
I've been suffering from anxiety ever since then
about all sorts of things
I've had depression for a long time
I'm always afraid
I've always kept to myself I am very nervous
I have chronic migraines

I have so many fears and phobias I don't understand
I was treated by a psychiatrist for years

I freeze whenever anyone wants to touch me
I can't stand massages
I feel afraid if anyone comes near if anyone comes too

close touches me I want to hit them

I've always been afraid of men and yet I've often
fallen for macho types violent
men who treated women like
shit
I have always had difficult complicated
painful relationships with men a while ago I
fell in love with a woman I am happy with her
and it's horrible to say this to say that this wonderful
relationship is partly because of him but I do think
there is a connection with what he did to me

I had forgotten everything but at a party when I was eighteen a
boy pinned me against a wall to kiss me it all
came back I collapsed to the ground

when the police called me three years ago I burst into
tears it plunged me back into something horrible
the incident came back to me when the police contacted me
it was buried inside me it all came back
when the police inspector called me

between the time when the Minors' Unit called me and when
I went there to update my report we wanted
to have a baby but I stopped ovulating I had panic
attacks again I was functioning in some kind of slow motion

232

the more I think about it the more traumatising it is
even though it was so very long ago

when I was pregnant I was so afraid of
contaminating my baby
during my two pregnancies it all came back to me again I
had serious neurological and heart problems
I'm constantly washing my children I panic very easily
especially since I've had children

my husband doesn't know
so coming to give evidence today was complicated
I don't want him to know
I wasn't able to tell my parents that he had been arrested
that there was a trial
I never told my husband
I invented an excuse to come today
it's the first time that I have spoken about it again in front of
other people

when I recognised him in the courtroom
it was a huge shock I was paralysed
the first day of the trial I did not recognise him from the back
but the moment he turned around
I had a knot in my stomach
he's the man I saw in the dock on the first day
– her whole body stiffens
it's him – nearly inaudible

I am a psychologist.
I practice martial arts, I became a boxer.
I am paediatrician in emergency medicine.
I am a law student, I would like to be a magistrate, maybe a children's judge.
I came here hoping it would help other people to avoid this.
I made the decision to come today to overcome my feelings of shame and guilt.

I would like to bring that day to a close.

The day after the one when you trapped us, we all woke up in our pretty childhood bedrooms and carried on, going to school, smiling and saying "thank you very much". We managed somehow, we were lucky, we were alive, it could have been worse. We never talked about it again, or we said very little. We each built our own existence. We did our best to keep it together, we stacked up difficult experiences and wonderful encounters on top of that day, the one we left in the basement, we forgot about it, we built walls, corridors, opened up windows, we lifted up the rafters with our own hands, and even if we felt confusedly that the construction had a flaw, we didn't know what it was, and so we learned how to fill the gaps and the panic attacks, how to keep the anguish out of sight in the attic. We invited guests over, we had the feeling that we were home at last.

After the call from the Minors' Unit, little black spots

appeared on our walls, we pressed them with the tips of our fingers, the walls flaked away. We looked at our doors, they were perforated by tunnels and galleries, we listened, and the walls, the floor, the ceiling started creaking, groaning, a bitter smell of excrement and saliva suddenly grabbed us. As we ran down the stairs, each step gave way beneath us in an opaque cloud, as soon as we were outside, the beautiful house that had cost us so much came crashing down. All at once.

Young women, nervous and naked, asking for justice to be done.

Marguerite, at nine years old, tells the police officers, "He put his willy into my front bottom and my back bottom, he hurt my front bottom, I started to cry, he put me back on the ground. Then he started again." Marguerite, whose pants were found to have sperm in them by the doctor from the Forensic Medical Unit she consulted the day of the events, who confirmed that there had been vaginal and anal penetration, Marguerite, who, when she is re-interviewed, three years ago, resists, balks, refuses to go through that day she had tried so desperately to forget, Marguerite says as little as possible and, during the investigation, Marguerite's case is downgraded from rape to sexual assault.

*

Philippine, to the captain, three years ago, "He put his finger in my vagina, I could feel that there was something going into it." Philippine, who is not advised that this is rape and that she is entitled to ask for a reclassification, Philippine, for whom sexual assault is time-barred, Philippine sees her request to join as a civil claimant denied.

Mathilda, also to the captain, three years ago, "I have the sensation of fingers going in between my labia." Mathilda, who when giving evidence describes how she remembers his fingers inside her, and whose barrister I wished would leap into the air to inform the jurors that this was rape, that Giovanni Costa will only be charged with sexual assault if her case isn't reclassified.

Juliette, who was one of the first to join as a civil claimant, Juliette suddenly stops speaking in the witness box, loses her train of thought, doesn't know anymore, Juliette, whose initial complaint of sexual assault is dismissed as time-barred, and whose counsel asks for a reclassification as attempted rape, Juliette receives this terrible salvo from the Presiding Judge: "Inadmissible conclusions, definitive dismissal order, case dismissed, termination of the public prosecution with respect to your claim!" That dispassionate Judge, who seemed so unaffected by Costa's insults, that unflappable man flushes crimson just this once. She annoys him, this

Juliette, telling us the long story of her life of pain, with her desperately smooth face, her air of detachment and her monotonous voice. The Bailiff comes to ask me to comfort her during the adjournment, and her inertia exasperates me too, I want to give her a shake. I forget that I should see this indifference as another signpost: the more a person is dissociated and emotionally anaesthetised, then the more she will have been exposed to serious violence, and the more danger she is in of being exposed to it again. That afternoon, I took her absence for a lack of understanding, I judged her severely, I did not recognise her.

Julia, whose sexual assault is time-barred, Julia, who has come to be a witness just the same, who was determined to do so, Julia bursts into tears when she speaks of the months that followed, when she was terrified at the idea of going out alone. A terror that has never left her.

Legal terms are powerless in describing hate. In one witness statement after another, twenty years later, no matter what he did to them, all of them are broken in pieces.

And as for me, after resolving not to mention the forced fellatio or his digital anal penetration, or his moist penis in my tiny mouth or his fat fingers in my anus, but to stick to my deposition from three years ago, so that my evidence doesn't lose credibility, I go no further than slipping in that I now know that other things happened too.

And Laura's statement, dating from 2003, regarding the rape of a minor alleged to have been committed by Giovanni Costa in 1983, and therefore time-barred, which the Prosecutor includes in his arguments. Twenty years were necessary for this woman to find the strength to enter a police station and file a report.

How many, like her, were never heard by their families? How many women are there, who have carried you all these years absolutely alone, Giovanni?

FOUR DAYS HAVE GONE by, and now I find myself loving the starched ceremony of the Assizes Court, the judges' and magistrates' long red gowns, the ermine, the barristers' long black gowns, the gendarmes, the refined language and the consecrated phrases. I love the benches with the high dark wooden backs that allow me to hide my face from the court when I feel overwhelmed. I love the scales, the fasces, the eye, the axe, the hand of justice, those intertwined plaster symbols that dominate the courtroom. I love the discreet support of the upset and silent gendarmes and their awkward gentleness towards us, I love the equally sudden and conspicuous sisterhood now woven between all the victims, the intelligence and humanity of the Prosecutor who is constantly seeking precision, pointing out issues, making things clear. I love the improvised picnics in the grand marble hallway under the eye of a bronze justice, her right hand held high, the tablets of the law held close to her heart, I love the different visitors who take turns to support me every day. I love it when my sister suddenly comes to give me a big hug, I love it that this trial is also somehow the trial of the seducer who disfigured her life. I love seeing my aunt, in the public seating area, asking who is whose mother, I love listening with one ear to my father chatting about Georgia with the counsel for the defence, I love feeling my mother desperately straining her ears to hear the Prosecutor. And I love the sunny afternoon, when my aunt takes the opportunity of an adjournment to take us to visit the Sainte-Chapelle, the soft serenity of the blue stained glass in the heart of chaos. I love my husband's unsteady and precise notes, his tender messages, his embraces. I love seeing the faces of the jurors lose their composure, as the witness statements follow each other, I love how their masks sink, how the bags under their eyes get deeper as the trial goes on, I love those jurors who sometimes dare to look at us, to show us, with just a flicker of their eyelids, their empathy, their humanity.

As I love, as I cry, I claim some of the space-time of Justice as my own. Here, where all my existence is contained in a few words, here where I will always be nine years old, here where the chaos of the world becomes order, where horror is qualified, here, at last, I feel sheltered, I have no need to pretend, I reassemble myself, I resemble myself at last.

*

On this morning of the fifth day, it is the court-appointed psychologists' turn to give expert evidence. Those who assessed the civil claimants, those who assessed the Accused.

The first one to address the court is the one who wiped the floor with me a year and a half ago, and I'm dreading what she has to say. She saw three of us.

She links the first victim's "psychological fragility, her neurotic profile, her fragile identity" to something completely different to the rape, to a serious accident or a death in the family. She says she only presents a "very mild" case of P.T.S.D. And yet this woman, when she was giving evidence in tears, described how Giovanni Costa plunged her into a profound state of traumatic immobilisation, how she hardly remembered anything, how she didn't understand how there could be sperm in her pants, how she couldn't remember having seen his penis, but how later, at nine years old, she would see erect penises appearing as if superimposed on all the men she came across. She suffered two periods of deep depression. As a young girl, she had been the victim of serious sexual violence again, first gang sexual assaults, then rape. She described being always on the lookout, every second, and how, as the trial approached, her sexuality was again destroyed.

The second one is me, and while she irritates me by describing my family and my studies in detail, what she says afterwards is restorative: "Severe state of P.T.S.D., compatible with the alleged facts." Why such a difference in diagnosis? Because I was prepared for the assessment, I had been helped to make the connections and to understand the damage for which he was the sole person responsible, I was trained not to minimise anything, not to apologise anymore.

The third one is Sybille, twenty-one years old and beauty to spare. Sybille, in tears, her powerful body curled up on the civil claimants' benches, her body that trembled so much that even today my hands remember it. Sybille, who would later say, "He completely destroyed me, I live in constant fear." The psychologist doesn't diagnose P.T.S.D. with her, because "in her case, the repression syndrome is stronger than the repetition syndrome". What does that even mean? She doesn't bother to explain it to the jurors.

At the end of her presentation, of all the people who gave evidence, she is the only one who is accorded a sympathetic aside by the Presiding Judge, "I know how your profession is being shaken up at the moment." And she replies, sweeping invisible flies away with the back of her hand, "We are on the side of Ethics."

The second expert psychologist is three hours late, charmed by his claimant and full of praise for her: never has he seen "such a successful psychological recovery", her "considerable intellectual faculties" mean she apparently has "no resulting psychological trauma", is "virtually recovered", the consequences on her life are "close to nil today".

Her barrister contests this. "Really? And yet she hasn't stopped crying since the beginning of the trial, she hangs on to her therapy sessions as if they were a lifesaver!"

And the expert argues, justifies himself, "The assessment subjects the victim to a reactivation, an imposed micro-trauma, and one has to be attentive to the way she organises her personality, I maintain my diagnosis." The Prosecutor perseveres, talks about traumatic amnesia and traumatic memory and the expert becomes tangled up in muddled explanations.

How ugly ignorance is when it is concealed under learned airs.

What a disgrace it is that doctors, psychologists, police officers and judges in France are not systematically trained in the specific symptoms of sexual violence.

When we know that, if a victim of sexual violence is correctly identified, diagnosed and treated, she can recover.

Then it's the turn of the expert psychologists who met Giovanni Costa. We are desperate to know what they will say, having had nothing but a vacant chair in an empty dock and the thousand grotesque characters that were projected onto it: Costa the Italian, the stallion, the man with steel balls, Costa the racegoer, the gambler, the man with pedicured feet and crocodile shoes, Costa the gentleman burglar, the itinerant international criminal, Costa the poor old man accused with no grounds, the victim of a conspiracy, Costa the loner, the outsider, Costa the rabid brute foaming with insults, Costa the old pervert, the satyr handing out lollies at the school gates, Costa the ogre, devouring tender little girls, Costa the sick, Costa the crazy, Costa the antisocial. Who is Costa?

None of them is familiar to me. None of them resembles the one who took up residence inside of me so long ago. No, the man I know, I recognised his traits in the other girls' evidence, I found his face again in his sniggering, his attacks and his upside-down words.

The first psychologist is on leave, she told the Registrar she would not be coming in. The Presiding Judge reads her report, she has concluded that he has a "paranoid organisation of his personality". Really? I know him to be too clever to believe his own hocus-pocus.

The girl who was at the same middle school as me did not come to the trial, but I meet her shortly afterwards. She is a psychologist. She is not angry at him, "Poor thing, he's a sociopath, an antisocial personality, he's sick." She is mostly mad at the police for not arresting him sooner. I bristle. I can't stand it when people say that, it's not enough for me. It doesn't make it easier for me in any way.

It doesn't tally with what I know about him in the depths of my being. He doesn't act impulsively, he doesn't throw himself at us, he waits. Patiently, for days on end. He chooses the child, the place, the scenario, he approaches beneath a mask, he kindly says the lying words, "My wife is pregnant, I have two children who are nine and ten years old, I'm looking for a room for my big boy, I'm sorry to have to ask you, I really need help." He methodically lays his trap, he instils terror drop by drop, then he uses us sexually, and the more he degrades us, the more he sniggers, the more he triumphs. When we are dissociated, confused, at his mercy, he says the poisonous words, the double-edged words, "You like it/ minx, I can see you love it/pig, it makes you so beautiful/ slag, it feels good/whore, you like it don't you, you do like it/pervert, you feel better, don't you/little slut, you were made for this/putana, you are a greedy girl/my bitch." And to finish off, the words that will lock us up, "It's our secret, I am your friend, it's just between you and me, don't tell anyone about it, they won't under-stand, promise me you will never tell, you're a good girl, here, to say thank you for helping me, I'll give you ten-twenty-thirty francs, lollies, an ice-cream."

*

A second expert is called to give evidence. And his words sound true, his words are restorative. "The responsibility of the Accused for the events is entire and complete. There is no psychiatric basis for a reduction or abolition of any potential sentence.

"He apparently presents a persecution complex of a paranoid type, but since it is exceptional that a person presenting this type of personality disorder commits rapes, this is probably an attempt at manipulation.

"It must be taken into consideration that we are dealing here with an extraordinarily malignant manipulator, a fact that is corroborated by the exceptional number of victims. I remind you that in France, in what is called the 'black number' of victims of sexual violence, an estimated ninety per cent of the victims of rape do not report it, and this number is even higher for child victims. In this case, you have identified seventy-two young victims, you might as well add a zero."

In the icy silence that follows, the Presiding Judge declares an adjournment before hearing the oral arguments of the barristers for the civil claimants.

My barrister comes towards me, she is holding seven pages of twelve-point text close to her chest, seven painful and secret pages, the distillation of the worst moments of my existence. She had asked me to select the passages from my sky blue notebooks that might make my suffering over so many years palpable to the jury. Before presenting them in writing to the court, she would like to read a few lines. "Oh no! That is out of the question. My mother, my sister, and my aunt are here. I don't want them to hear that, it was not meant for them."

But then there is Marguerite, there is Sybille, there is Leïla, there are all these innumerable girls, these wonderful, brave girls who took their turn in the witness box, there is our suffering, denied by the Sunday-afternoon experts, and so "yes", and so "alright". I run out towards the grand marble corridor, I run to see my mother, my sister, my aunt. "I'm so sorry, my barrister is going to read my diaries, I didn't want you to hear this, those words were not meant for you, please forgive me – I love you."

My barrister starts reading, I bury myself in my seat, I am ashamed that everyone is hearing my ugliness laid bare.

At the end of the reading, I stare fixedly at my hands, overwhelmed, making sure I don't make eye contact with anyone. My aunt, my darling aunt, comes from behind to bury her head in my shaking shoulder and to clasp me in her arms. "We are all so clueless, we never understood a thing."

*

The Presiding Judge reads the questions which the jurors will have to answer. Eighty-four principal questions, twenty-three subsidiary questions. He has made sure for each victim, that if Giovanni Costa is not found guilty of either rape or sexual assault, he can still be convicted of attempted rape or attempted sexual assault.

The oral arguments of the barristers for the fourteen civil claimants begin. Each of them employs such a particular style that you would think that the parade of long black gowns was a demonstration of courtroom practice:

The roaring man, pointing at the empty dock, "I'm asking you to obliterate that man!"

The creator of fine phrases, she's the media's favourite.

The competent, vivacious woman, "In front of the child is a double barrier, first being heard by her parents, then that her parents report the crime. The women who appear in court today are also appearing for those who are absent, for all those little girls he met during a long career devoted to doing evil."

The disengaged woman, the one who spent the whole trial sending text messages, the one who had better things to do with her time.

The astounded, emotional man, "My client, married and the mother of two children, confided to me that she had never had sexual relations to which she fully consented."

The technical guy, the lover of articles of the law.

And the volcanic woman, whose lightning-fast argument comes crashing down and closes the day's proceedings with a flourish.

ON THE MORNING OF the sixth day, as I arrive, the gendarmes warn me: Costa is there. The Presiding Judge briefs the barristers for the civil claimants who haven't yet presented their arguments, he warns them that the first one to speak will face a volley of abuse, and that they mustn't let it get to them. He lets them decide who goes first.

My husband is sitting up straight next to me, I need all our love to contain my fear.

He comes into the dock, he doesn't look at us, he puts on a courteous little smile for the Presiding Judge and the jurors, then sits down. All eyes are fixed upon him, when will he start shouting? A barrister advances towards him, addresses him, scrutinises him, glares at him, gets him into a corner, charges at him, and then, nothing. He doesn't respond. He sits quietly. He sits quietly, but he is there, listening, and the words are changed, the words start to build, to bandage, to straighten, all it takes is for him to be present at last, sitting in the dock, with us on the victims' benches, for the words to be in their right places, for justice to be done.

Another barrister is addressing the court, I don't hear her, you are glaring at me, Giovanni, and all of me is occupied in holding your gaze, in not dissociating this time, in breathing, in feeling my anger boil up while your piercing eyes try to lower mine. You look away at last, and in that minuscule triumph, I find the threshold of my new life to come.

The last barrister for the prosecution, a charismatic, bellicose tenor, concludes the arguments with "These little girls later poured concrete, poured lead, on top of all of this, but it kept rotting away underneath, it poisoned their whole lives."

Giovanni Costa comes back after lunch, I have to pinch myself to believe it.

The Prosecutor rises up, immense, he is no longer hunched over the little microphone, but looming over the Accused. He locks eyes with him and starts his indictment: "Monsieur Costa, you have either been absent, or outrageous and insulting, but you are required to answer the charges laid against you." He has the long red gown with the ermine collar, and a clear, lively delivery,

"Monsieur Costa, nineteen victims have come to be witnesses, you have not deigned to hear them."

Costa does not lower his head, he keeps eye contact, he mumbles, "get fucked, you scum", his jaws are locked and his lips are white, but I am nine years old and, in the stairwell, a handsome young red knight with tortoiseshell glasses has risen up, a great avenger bedecked in ermine, Saint George of Lydda with his long lance, so you can go spit, you demon.

The Prosecutor gives details of each case, victim by victim, I am second, he takes my little girl's photograph printed in A4, my timid smile, my round collar and my freckles, and brandishes me in front of Costa. "Remember this child, this child you raped."

Costa leaps up, his fist raised, his face tumescent, all swollen with hatred, he screams, "That child, you're the one who raped her, arsehole! You're the child rapist, you scum!" And even though at that moment I am nothing but terror curled up on a wooden bench, I recognise that violence, I know it by heart, that violence was what mutilated me for all those years, that ugliness, I can see it outside of myself at last, and, liberated, I sit up straight again. My burning tears evaporate before they even start to flow.

The Presiding Judge orders him to calm down, he sits down again, but as soon as the Prosecutor talks about Marguerite, trembling and dignified, her hands laced with mine, he vituperates, he spits, he sneers, and when

Clara's turn comes, "It's all lies! I was in Germany, in Düsseldorf! This is a scandal! I'm going to the press with this! Go fuck yourself!" The gendarmes grab him and drag him still sputtering towards the exit.

"We are dealing with someone addicted to violence, who will certainly reoffend. For all these lives reduced to nothingness, I seek twenty years of incarceration, the maximum allowed by the law."

That evening I go to a concert, I sing at the top of my voice, I dance, I drink caipirinhas, the music goes through me and moves me, I dance, I am immense and infinite, I vibrate, I am in bliss, I turn a chorus into a mantra, "you'll be fine, you'll see", I sing it all the time, I make it my banner, I embroider it into each of my thoughts, this last night, I get drunk on alcohol and hope.

THE SEVENTH AND LAST day. Giovanni Costa is here.

It is Counsel for the defence's turn to address the court. They aren't Secrétaires de la Conférence for nothing, and since we're in the Victor Hugo courtroom, they all drop a citation from *The Last Day of a Condemned Man*. Their speeches are beautiful and well phrased. "A man's trial is the time for his reintegration into society rather than his repudiation." They insist that he be judged as a human being and not as a monster, and since "the scales of Justice have been unbalanced by this empty dock", the more pugnacious of the two barristers attempts to unravel the tight fabric of accusations.

In the Assizes Court, the Accused has the final word. An allotted time to speak which no-one is allowed to interrupt and whose length is determined by the Presiding Judge, who keeps his eyes fixed on the scales.

Giovanni Costa rises, smiles. He addresses the court for the first time. In a Franco-Italian pidgin that is difficult to follow, he talks about Pétain, wasps, Cardinal Mazarin, real Italian pasta, Garibaldi, the restoration of antique furniture, Mussolini, his life as a burglar, he talks without drawing breath, he jumps from one idea to the next, he gambols, he's having fun, but I need him to take account of what he has done to us, and with two other victims, I stand up, facing him, hoping to make him react, but nothing, not a startle, not a look, he continues, imperturbable, all-powerful, he's playing, he rants on with his history of France for idiots, I can't stand it anymore, I flee the courtroom, I run into the grand marble hallway, I run and my legs give way and I fall. On all fours, I'm sobbing and my tears are black.

Embraced, lifted up, supported by my aunt and my barrister, I pull myself together and slide back onto the wooden bench in silence to endure more of his sardonic, erratic nonsense, his apotheosis.

Every time the Presiding Judge orders him to return to the facts, he is indignant. "I don't look like a sadist or a rapist," he protests. "No-one rapes two- or three-year-old babies in Italy." Or he details the contents of a suitcase he left in that hotel in Düsseldorf.

And when, at the end of forty interminable minutes, the Judge asks him to conclude at last, he goes all solemn, "Mesdames and Messieurs of the jury, Monsieur le Président, I'm sorry, I say this with all my heart: I am not a rapist." We all perk up at "I'm sorry", but in vain, there's no hope, it's nothing but an Italian tic, a *prego*, a nothing word.

The proceedings are over. The Presiding Judge, the Assessor Judges and the jurors retire for deliberations.

Over the course of these seven days we have spent together, I have examined the drawn expressions of compassion on their faces, I've wanted, a hundred times, to join them for a cigarette on the steps of the Palais, but we all kept to our places, we did not venture to the limits of the law, and now there is nothing left to say, it's up to them to decide.

Strange hours, those spent waiting for a judgment, wandering through the too-elegant streets of the centre of Paris, feeling the magnetic pull of the Palais and its jurors sequestered inside, clutching my mobile like a pregnancy test.

And you, Giovanni? What did you do? What, or who did you think about? Who are you, in the closed silence of a cell, when no-one is looking at you?

It is over. Earlier than the Registrar predicted. Six hours of deliberations for one hundred and seven questions, they didn't waste their time. My father jumps into a taxi, my aunt onto her bike, and a crowd of girls you wanted to annihilate, Giovanni, all converge on the

Victor Hugo courtroom in a rush. We have all come to hear the verdict.

Another hour waiting for the Accused's barristers, who are unreachable, an hour going round in circles, trying to exhaust anticipation. The Defence arrive at last. We rise. The jurors enter.

Giovanni Cost is found guilty.
Of everything.
Eighteen years in prison.

We fall into each other's arms, we smile great big timid smiles at each other. It has been so long, so many days, months, years, that I have been sitting on this wooden bench waiting for the announcement of my liberation. Now it's your turn to be locked up, Giovanni, your turn to carry all the weight of your hatred.

You are standing up, very straight, your chin held high, your eyes like steel marbles, and now your accent has completely disappeared, your elocution is clear, the words you pronounce have surgical clarity. "Excuse me, Monsieur le Président, since you are the instigator of my defeat, make sure you wipe your ass with it properly tonight, in your boyfriend's bed."

FIVE DAYS LATER, I receive a registered letter. Giovanni Costa lodged an appeal, alone, without consulting his lawyers, the night of the verdict, as soon as he arrived at the prison office.

I try not to fall apart, so he doesn't have that victory. I fall apart anyway. I don't have the heart to start again. I don't have the heart to wait two or three more years for a new Assizes Court in another *département* to be designated, to find myself alone in an unfamiliar city, to stand naked again in front of unknown jurors. I have my life to live, it's been waiting for me for so long.

But I will go, and I will encourage all the victims I know to come again too. Without our trembling evidence, our breaking voices, our faces pulled tight with held-back tears, without us, the horror of the crime will be muted and the criminal will triumph. When jurors are not affected, they are more lenient. I will go.

I had hoped, naively, that the Presiding Judge would take the opportunity of this trial to advance the cause of victims of sexual violence. I hoped in vain. He knows about all our torn lives. He heard about all its long-term consequences, in one evidence statement after the other. He knows that Costa is insolvent and that the amounts he will be sentenced to pay to the civil claimants "in reparation for the damages suffered" will only be symbolic. He knows that symbols are restorative, he knows the power of his long red gown trimmed with ermine, he knows the impact of the words he pronounces. No matter, he does no more than stick to the old jurisprudence, conform to the established amounts – fifteen thousand euros for rape, seven thousand for sexual assault. In France, you can destroy a woman's life for the price of a second-hand car.

To one of us, whose story is neither more nor less terrifying, neither more nor less sordid, he grants twice that amount. Why? No-one knows, these decisions do not need to be justified. Did he find her more moving? More deserving of the consideration of the State? Does her life have a higher price? Suffering is not enough, we have to deserve the empathy we are shown.

We all appeal his decisions, except her. He has managed to divide us.

This morning on a public radio station, a comedian making a list of first sexual experiences adds an uncle "who was a bit of a pest". Ha ha ha. I turn the radio off. When will we stop confusing sexuality with violence, sexual desire with addiction to stress, consent with the freeze response? What that child experienced is not sexuality, but hatred, ugliness, and the abuse of power. Nothing in common with pleasure, embraces, caresses, nothing, absolutely nothing, with the fusion of bodies.

Epilogue

YOUR BODY IS COLD. You died that day, in the merry month of May, and there is nothing I can do to give your breath back to you. I thought writing would allow me to find you again, one sentence at a time, to save you, and that all it would take was a kiss on your forehead to wake you up. But your face is blue and I don't know how to embrace you. And so I talk to you, like you used to talk to Grand-Père, under the plum tree. All these years, you have been waiting for me, you knew that as I made my way towards you, I would find myself. I am laying down this book before you, so these paper flowers can be your crown.

The harm he did to you is inside me, it does not go away, it is a black granite boulder in the middle of a meadow. Now I can see it, now I can remember, and I can play, and rollick and romp with my son until we fall down exhausted with laughter and tickles in the waving grass, and nothing is more foreign to me than yesterday's images. Sometimes, I embrace the man I love and our bodies exult, and nothing else exists between us except the Joy of being in the world.

Life never lets go, in the ocean depths, in the shadows, it glows.

In my mouth, in my throat, the fireworks of an apple crunching in my teeth. In my nostrils, down my windpipe, the smell of pine needles rolling between my fingertips. In the palms of my hands, the moist, vibrant warmth of fistfuls of rich earth.

AFTERWORD

Giovanni Costa's appeal was set down for January 2018. Many victims who had not been able to attend the trial that had taken place in the Assizes Court were present, some having travelled long distances from other countries. The first morning was gruelling, with the Accused continually interrupting the proceedings: he was having dizzy spells, he had back pain, he claimed he didn't understand what was being asked of him. During the lunch break, the Presiding Judge of the Court of Appeal requested an expert medical assessment. On our return, we learned that Giovanni Costa's state of health was not compatible with continuing the trial, and that in consequence the appeal would be adjourned *sine die*. On the benches for the civil claimants, our bodies broke down as he fixed us with his triumphant, icy glare. A final thrust of the dagger.

In October 2018, a further expert medical opinion found new grounds to stay the appeal.

Under French law, Giovanni Costa will therefore be presumed innocent for the rest of his life, but he will remain in prison as a preventative measure. At the moment of his death, the appeal not having taken place, he will, at last, be judged guilty.

AB, December 2018

I HAVE CHANGED THE names of the other victims, but they were always with me as I was writing this book, and they were the ones who gave me the courage to keep going.

Thank you to Muriel Salmona, my doctor of marine botany and archaeology.

Thank you to my barrister, Maître Agnès Cittadini, for her fervour, competence and humanity.

Thank you to my family and friends, to everyone who offered me their confidence, tenderness, laughter and love.

ADÉLAÏDE BON is a French writer, actress and voice artist. She graduated from the École supérieure d'art dramatique in Paris, and in parallel, completed five years of training on issues of gender equality, learning the techniques of the Theatre of the Oppressed, under the auspices of a feminist company, partnered with the European Association Against Violence Against Women, and the Mémoire Traumatique association led by Dr Muriel Salmona. She lives in Paris. *The Little Girl on the Ice Floe* is her first book.

RUTH DIVER is the winner of the 2016 *Asymptote* Close Approximations Fiction Prize for her translation of *Maraudes* by Sophie Pujas, and of two French Voices Awards in 2017, for *Marx et la poupée* by Maryam Madjidi, and *Titus n'aimait pas Bérénice* by Nathalie Azoulai. She collaborated with Ros Schwartz on the translation of *The Reader on the 6.27* by Jean-Paul Didierlaurent. She has a PhD from the University Paris 8 and the University of Auckland, New Zealand, where she was the Head of Comparative Literature until 2014. *The Little Girl on the Ice Floe* is her first full-length translation.